WHAT OTHERS

Real Issues, Real Teens! addresse A necessity for parents who desire to

—Eastman Curtis, Senior Pastor of Destiny Church; host of two award-winning television shows, This Generation *and* Destiny TV. *Author of several books, including* You Can Make It Happen, Raising Heaven Bound Kids in a Hell Bent World, Xtreme Talk, *and* Every Day I Pray for My Teenager. *His radio devotionals can be heard on over 500 radio stations around the world.*

T. Suzanne Eller's newest book is certain to be a tremendous help to parents everywhere who want to know what their teens are really thinking. Good communication is key to any healthy relationship, but it's especially important in the parent-teen relationship. Thanks to Suzie Eller's transparency with her own parenting struggles, her love and concern for today's youth, and the invaluable insight provided by teenagers themselves, this book will no doubt go a long way toward healing hurting families.

—Martha Bolton, Emmy- and Dove-nominated writer and author of over fifty books, including If the Tongue's a Fire, Who Needs Salsa? Cool Advice for Hot Topics from the Book of James

In *Real Issues, Real Teens!* author T. Suzanne Eller has hit the target as she articulates the heart and cry of this generation of youth. Her insights and practical advice make this book a must-read for parents, youth workers, and all who care about teens.

—Cheri Fuller, speaker and award-winning author of thirty books, including When Teens Pray: Powerful Stories of How God Works, When Mothers Pray: Bringing God's Power and Blessing to Your Children's Lives, *and* The Mom You're Meant to Be

I can't rave enough about this book. My only complaint is, "Why wasn't this book published when my kids were teens?" This book will empower you to be the parent of teens that you really want to be. It's insightful, motivating, powerful, revealing, and honest. Got teens? Get this book! It's a must.

—Kathy Collard Miller, conference speaker and author of numerous books, including Princess to Princess: Your Inheritance as a Daughter of the King, The Un-Devotional for Teens: Fun Puzzles to Help You Learn Scripture, *and* Staying Friends With Your Kids

As a volunteer youth worker for over twenty years (and a parent for almost twenty-five), I read *Real Issues, Real Teens!* with great interest. I was encouraged, challenged, and convicted as I heard directly from these teenagers. Thanks to Suzie and to the youth who so honestly helped me to more fully "get it."

—Kendra Smiley, international speaker and author of several books, including Empowering Choices: Inspiring Stories to Encourage Godly Decisions *and* Helping Your Kids Make Good Choices: Guiding Your Children in a World Full of Options, Encouraging Parents of All Ages and Stages

As a Christian counselor, I see many parents struggle to understand their teenager. Suzie Eller gifts us with an encyclopedia of sound wisdom and heartfelt challenges so that we might comprehend their world and guide them successfully through the murky waters of adolescence. *Real Issues, Real Teens!* will find a prominent place in my waiting room.

—Leslie Vernick, DCSW, LCSW, Director of Christ Centered Counseling, author of How to Find Selfless Joy in a Me-First World.

This book should come with a warning label! Parents must avoid it if they're unwilling to take an instructive look at teens today. From one who works with and specializes in teen ministry, author, Suzanne Eller gives hopeful and helpful information that can improve the parent/teen relationship and ultimately home life. She sums it up best with, "Sometimes we place our loved ones in God's hands as we work on the only people we can really change—ourselves." Educational and enlightening, *Real Issues, Real Teens!* is not all complaints and criticism about parents. It includes positive, affirming answers straight from teens themselves of what parents are doing right. Find out now, if you dare.

—Brenda Nixon, M.A., speaker, educator, author of Parenting Power in the Early Years

What Teens Are Saying

I hope parents actually read this book and realize that we did say these things and we weren't paid to be honest. Maybe they'll realize that we have good intentions that don't always come out right. Maybe they can understand more about my generation.

—Janelle T., age 15

There are many things I can't tell my mom face-to-face. This book will give her the chance to realize what I want and need from her. She might not understand if I told her straight out.

—Lara M., age 16

I appreciate people like Suzie who actually talk to us and care about what's going on in our lives.

—Melissa M., age 15

I think that this is a great idea, having the kids say what they see and what they think instead of always getting the adult view about what should be done. I really believe that this book will help a lot of people see their children or teens differently.

—Sarah A., age 15

This is a cool idea for a book. I hope this book works. They are right when they say we are a disconnected generation. I know I'm disconnected.

—Mercy D., age 15

It's been great to answer these questions. I never realized how close I was to my parents until now. This is an awesome idea for a book.

—Selena B., age 18

I think this is an excellent idea. Parents will be able to hear from real teens and realize how they are helping or hurting their teens. It will probably also open up a whole new door and give parents insight as to how we feel in this day and age. I think that this book will give hope to teens and parents as we begin to understand each other.

—Adam D., age 18

Real Issues, Real Teens!

Real Issues, Real Teens!

What Your Teen Really Wants from You

T. Suzanne Eller

An Imprint of Cook Communications Ministries
COLORADO SPRINGS, COLORADO • PARIS, ONTARIO
KINGSWAY COMMUNICATIONS, LTD., EASTBOURNE, ENGLAND

Life Journey® is an imprint of
Cook Communications Ministries, Colorado Springs, CO 80918
Cook Communications, Paris, Ontario
Kingsway Communications, Eastbourne, England

REAL ISSUES, REAL TEENS!

First Printing, 2004
Printed in the United States of America
1 2 3 4 5 6 7 8 9 10 Printing/Year 08 07 06 05 04

Published in association with the literary agency of Janet Kobobel Grant, 4788 Carissa Avenue, Santa Rosa, CA 95405.

Cover Design: Marks & Whetstone

The names of the teens in this book have been changed to protect their identities.

Library of Congress Cataloging-in-Publication Data

Eller, T. Suzanne.
Real issues, real teens!: what your teen really wants from you / T. Suzanne Eller.
p. cm.
Includes bibliographical references and index.
ISBN 0-7814-4058-0 (pbk.)
1. Teenagers–Religious life. 2. Teenagers–Conduct of life. 3. Family–Religious life. 4. Parent and teenager. I. Title.
BV4447.E55 2004
248.8'45–dc22

2003023228

Dedicated to Melissa, Ryan and Leslie.
Not just my kids, but people who inspire me.
I'm so lucky to be your mom.

Contents

Foreword 13
Acknowledgments 17
Introduction 19
Chapter One—Please Listen to Me 23
Chapter Two—Reality Check 43
Chapter Three—Your Teen's Cluster 83
Chapter Four—How's Your Day? 95
Chapter Five—Show, Not Tell 123
Chapter Six—It's a Trust Issue 139
Chapter Seven—Home Sweet Home 159
Chapter Eight—Do You Have a Minute? 183
Chapter Nine—What You Teach Me about God 197
Chapter Ten—Relevant Family Faith 223
Chapter Eleven—Restoring Broken Relationships 253
Chapter Twelve—If I Could Tell You One Thing 275
Notes 283

Foreword

There is a fresh movement of God these days. You can feel it. God is doing something new and fresh in the hearts and minds of students today. Step into churches and conference centers, Starbucks and college classrooms—and you can feel it.

This generation, perhaps in greater measure than any before it, is open to the spiritual. They hunger for it. They yearn for it. They are searching for the spiritual—something that is bigger and more transcendent than themselves—something to satisfy the hunger. They know that life is more than what they've seen or tasted. "Is this all there is?" is their cry. They are searching—but they're not finding it in our churches.

You see, that's the problem.

Most students today are searching for the spiritual, some peace or sense of the presence of "God." Yet most of them are not looking in our homes or our churches. In fact, they are fleeing from our homes and churches. They seem to be searching and finding their spiritual answers in the modern-day prophets of the media—songwriters are the new prophets, film directors the new priests. Media is now the porthole into a new spiritual realm. Sometimes it is amazingly fresh and authentic, sometimes not.

We have a choice to make.

We can continue down the way of the path that is being created for us or we can choose differently. It would be so easy for us as parents to throw our hands up and say there is nothing we can do. We feel ill-equipped. We feel inadequate.

We feel so much less than we think we need to be. So we remain silent.

We have another choice.

I am amazed time and again at the ancient texts of our faith. The Scriptures are letters, poems, prayers, and collections of writings and stories written by real people to real people, inspired by the living God. The Scriptures are not "God's little answer book" to all the issues and problems of life. It is not a field manual—unfolding for us what to do in the event of any and every emergency. The Scriptures are the ancient and holy writings of the people of God—written as they struggled to find him and live in harmony with him.

This struggle took place when the people of God were about to come into the Promised Land. They had been in the desert—not of their own accord, but because God wanted to shape in them a new identity. They needed to leave behind the identity of slaves and take on a new identity—the people of God. As they passed through the desert their identity as slaves was scorched away, burned away with the blowing of the hot wind in their faces.

It is at this point, on the edge of the Promised Land, that Moses sends the twelve spies into the land. Ten come back with the report that there are giants in the land—a land that devours its people. Two have another idea.

"The land we passed through and explored is exceedingly good. If the Lord is pleased with us, he will lead us into that land, a land flowing with milk and honey, and will give it to us. Only do not rebel against the Lord. And do not be afraid of the people of the land, because we will swallow them up. Their protection is gone, but the LORD is with us. Do not be afraid of them" (Num. 14:7–9).

We have a choice to make.

My hope for us is that we choose not to do what our spiritual predecessors did—run away from the culture and hide in the fortress walls of the church. May we do what Jesus did: reach out to our culture—engage it, interact with it, listen to it—and change it.

May you find in these pages comfort and uncomfortability. May you find the words of today's generation a challenge to you to reach out to your kids and to listen to them. May their words stir you … challenge you … captivate you … and change you—and so change them.

Mike DeVries
Pastor, communicator, author of *Partnering with Parents*
Mission Viejo, California

Acknowledgments

Every teen who filled out a survey or allowed me to interview him or her helped me write this book. You talked openly, and I learned so much from you. These interviews made me a better mom. They helped me to listen to the heartbeat of a generation waiting to be heard.

I want to thank the teens who are a part of my discipleship class. You guys allow me a glimpse into your world every week, and I love you. No matter how far I travel, I look forward to getting back home so I can sit and talk about God with you. I love the fact that you are seekers. I love it when you give me that look like, "Are you kidding me?" but take the plunge anyway. You keep me grounded and in touch. You absolutely rock!

I appreciate Pastors Andy and Sarah Greene, my home church youth pastors. I am so blessed to be a part of a team that is genuinely supportive and to work with two of the coolest youth pastors around. Thank you, Andy, for your kind words and for allowing me to be a part of such an amazing youth program. Thank you, Sarah, for your example of true class and compassion.

I'd like to thank the other members of the team, Brian and Amanda, Tabitha, Angelia, Kris, and Tiffany. You pour yourselves out every week, like an offering, to make a difference in the lives of youth. Second only to youth, I love hanging out with people who love teens. You guys are awesome.

I appreciate Terry Whalin and the team at Cook Communications Ministries. The author is only a small part of the process of creating a book. I appreciate those who shared in the birth of this project. Your fingerprints are all over it.

I want to thank Janet Kobobel Grant, who believed in me when I was just beginning to figure out that I could actually pursue my dream of being an author.

God has graciously given me friends and family who aren't afraid to share in this wild adventure, and the face that shines more brightly than any other is that of my husband, Richard. You work so hard so that I can follow the path God has placed before me. Thank you for living such an unselfish life. You are my example. Thank you for crying and laughing in all the right places when you read my writing. Thank you for being my soul mate. I'm blessed to have you in my life and heart.

Ryan, Leslie, and Melissa, thank you for loving me in spite of my mistakes. Thanks for allowing me to use personal stories in this book. I love the fact that we have graduated from parent-child relationships to friendships. I consider that a gift. Thanks for being such awesome human beings. I'm still learning, and you have been great teachers.

Introduction

Every Wednesday I walk into a youth service that is chaotic and loud—and sometimes it involves gross food games—but I love it. I worship with teens who run after God with a passion. I kneel with them as they weep over their failures and fears. Every Sunday I sit with a group of teens and teach an intense discipleship class. It is a blessing to work with youth as they seek a deeper faith relationship and explore what it means to be a disciple of Christ.

Whenever I hear negative things about this generation, I quickly rise to their defense. It's no secret that our teens are embattled, but the good news is that this generation is comprised of seekers. They live their faith in a bold, uncompromising fashion, and I firmly believe that this generation will rock our world for Christ.

Teens across the nation are tired of disrespect. They don't want to be labeled and lumped into a faceless group of no-gooders. They are speaking up and asking hard questions. They've heard, seen, and experienced things that their parents might not even feel comfortable talking about. They want traditional standards, but ones that make sense in their world and culture. They want faith, but they want it to be real. They want family, but family doesn't have to be a traditional one; it simply has to be a place where they can feel loved and accepted.

Teens want answers. They are looking for people to show them—not tell them—the truth. *Authenticity* is a new buzzword. Though teens may not agree with you, they respect the fact that someone—anyone—will live what he believes.

This book is a glimpse into teen culture and the hearts of teens. I interviewed hundreds of youth from all over the United States ranging in age from twelve to twenty-one. I asked hard questions such as: How can parents impact you in your faith? What do parents do that pushes you away from God? How can adults instill confidence and strength in you? What messages do you have for parents desperate to be a part of the world of their teens? I promised to listen to the teens without talking, without judgment, and without lectures—and they opened up!

Listening helped me to understand the errors I made in the past that discouraged my own children. One day I read a survey and I saw my own mistakes in it. That morning I sent my oldest daughter an e-mail with a long overdue apology. To be honest, I hadn't even seen my mistake until I saw it through a teen's eyes. My daughter was gracious, letting me know that she loved me and that she thought I was a good mom. She also told me that the clarity I had gained was awesome. These interviews and surveys not only brought insight to me as a mother, but they impacted my ministry as a speaker and a youth worker.

I learned that every teen longs to tell his parents that he loves them—even if it appears that he is pushing his parents away. I learned never to give up on a teen, no matter what the circumstances. There were several times that I put aside the book research and responded to the teen I was interviewing. Some answers on the surveys were revealing, and it was time to forget about the book for a moment and reach out.

Though I'm a mom of teens and have worked with teens for almost two decades (my goal is to be the world's oldest youth staff member), I want you to understand that I don't have all the answers. I know God has given me a burden for youth; however, this book is not about me, my wisdom, or my insights about teens. This book is about them. It's an open dialogue. If you are looking for a book that will show you how to be "Parent of the Year," you might want to put this down right now, because the following chapters will bring up more questions than answers. But that's good news, for questions create opportunity for real conversations.

This book is a chance for you to hear the voice of a generation that says parents are a huge influence—positive or negative. You will see through teens' eyes how your decisions shape them. This book will give you practical tools to impact your relationship with your teens by seeing their perspectives. Then you will have a chance to make it real by applying it to your own life.

You may not agree with everything that the teens have to say. There were times when I disagreed with them myself, and as I talked with these teens, I shared my view as a mom or as an adult on some issues. The important thing was that hearing their perspectives allowed us to talk about things that mattered to each of us and to see issues from each other's viewpoints.

I hear teens say all the time that they would give anything if their moms or dads would really listen to them. At the same time, I hear parents say that they long for their children to talk to them. There are thousands of parents desperate to connect with their teens. Is that you? Are you willing to listen to what teens are saying to the most influential people in their lives?

This is your chance.

Chapter One

Please Listen to Me

God speaks in the silence of the heart.
Listening is the beginning of prayer.
—Mother Teresa

Question: If your parents could do one thing to impact you, what would it be?

Having parents that will listen is such a blessing. I don't believe that keeping things pent up helps anything. If we can share our strife and joys without judgment, it makes a great deal of difference in our lives. It deepens the bond between us because we break that personal barrier.

Vickie M., age 21

Today's secular music reaffirms the cry of this generation.

The lyrics of one popular rock band ask parents, "Are my screams loud enough for you to hear?" Music is the poetry of every generation, and songs such as these tell us that teenagers long to be heard.

If my parents could do one thing, I'd tell them to listen to me, teach me, tell me what I should do.

Rebekah B., age 14

Today's youth culture is distinctly different than it was when we were teens. There was a time when parents were protectors of their children, but there has been a significant changing of the guard. Today's teens hide the harsh realities of their world from their parents, leaving adults in a state of innocence, shielded from the truth. We'll discuss these cultural changes later, but right now it is important to know that understanding the differences in your teen's world gains you nothing if there is a wall of silence between you.

How can you listen if your teen refuses to talk? Teens want to have a conversation, but they won't attempt it unless they know their parents will pay attention. They need to know that Mom or Dad is willing to listen. That means that parents need to stop talking long enough to hear what their children have to say.

My dad and I get along, and I love him. He is good to talk to. He doesn't ask questions. He just listens. That is what I like about talking to him.

Brianna B., age 16

Teenagers take huge risks when they are open with adults. How will an adult react or respond when the teens share their lives? Teens I interviewed shared five reasons why they don't talk with their parents.

REASON #1—MY PARENTS MIGHT NOT UNDERSTAND

Question: Do you ever hide the reality of your world from your parents? Why?

What I go through is so different from what they went through. The normalcy of school and behavior has changed. What I put up with every day would probably get to them even though I'm used to it.

Laura N., age 15

It's difficult for teens to tell a parent about someone at school having oral sex in the bathroom or what it's like to stand up for their faith in a culture that is increasingly hostile to Christianity. How do you put in plain words that you are the only virgin in your entire class? How can you tell your parents that you are considered intolerant when you try to express your beliefs? The biggest fear teens have about talking with an adult is not having to share the truth, but trying to express the truth without receiving judgment—not for what they do, but for their culture.

I don't tell them about my world because they wouldn't understand.

Gemma M., age 13

How would you react if your teen told you that a girl in her class was a lesbian? What would you do if your daughter told you that a friend had an abortion? Both of these situations are commonplace in your teen's culture, and yet your teen is trying to live out a faith that says that both of these decisions are sin.

My parents honestly have no clue what my day-to-day life is like.
Elizabeth B., age 17

Today's teens are attempting to show God's love in a culture that says that if they take a stand against these and other issues they are demonstrating hatred. Do you realize how difficult that is? You may not understand or agree with today's cultural views, but it's important to listen when your teens tell you what is going on. Too often, instead of finding assurance and encouragement from their parents, they receive something very different.

Church kids and unchurched kids think and act very similar. I know I'm dealing with a lot of problems that unchurched kids face too.

Stan T., age 15

In a discussion group, one sixteen-year-old girl shared her frustration. "My mom thinks that if I listen to Christian music and wear a Christian T-shirt and live in a Christian home, that I don't deal with the same things that my non-Christian friends do. That's simply not true." This teen tried to talk to her parents, but when she shared the details of her life they hyped up the list of Christian to-dos. "They thought if I did more Christian things that the world outside the church doors would disappear, I guess. I just needed someone to listen, and they refused to even try to hear what I was saying. They didn't understand that all I needed was their support."

Our teens need to know that there is someone who will

listen to what they have to say. Those conversations may be great opportunities to give them nudges in the right direction or encouragement that they are doing the right thing. Though we might not understand the world our teens live in, we can give them a safe place to land. That brings us to the next reason teens don't talk.

Reason #2—To Avoid a Lecture

My parents, despite what they believe, know very little of what really goes on in my life. It's not that I deliberately hide stuff from them because I'm scared of them finding out, but more because they would give lengthy lectures on how horrible the world is today. I keep things from my parents because it is easier to live and life goes smoother. It's not like I am trying to be sneaky or underhanded; it's just easier this way. Things I see and hear on the bus and at school would send them into conniptions, but it is just part of my day-to-day life.

Karianne P., age 17

Teens often fail to talk about their world in order to avoid a lecture on purity or a three-point sermon on strength in times of difficulty. Have you ever talked with someone and realized he wasn't listening but rather was formulating what he wanted to say to you? I have, and it's discouraging. I probably wouldn't pick that person to talk with on a deeper level a second time.

Too often parents fail to grasp what teens are saying because they are so eager to turn the conversations into life lessons. The result is a complete shutdown of communication. Most parents desire to guide and encourage their teens, but in order to do that, parents have to hear what their children are saying. Listening without speaking is the key to gaining entrance into our teens' lives. Listening without speaking gives parents the ability to eventually offer realistic encouragement and support because they actually know what is going on. This then allows the parents to carry a portion of the burden for their teens as they make critical daily decisions.

Actually, I am really honest with my parents. I am always open to talk to them about anything. There have been some incidents where I was afraid of how they would react and I waited to tell them. Even in the times I just tell them no matter how I think they will react, I know they will always love me and be there for me.

Jezel C., age 16

How do you react when your teen talks to you? Do you instantly respond with advice? Put any lectures on the shelf as you listen the whole way to the end, allowing your teen to share the entire story. Ask questions that help her to work through the problem.

On one occasion I received a phone call from a distraught teen. She was a nineteen-year-old college student who was dating a seventeen-year-old high school senior who had cheated on her with another girl who was now pregnant. As this student talked, the details of her story got messier. She had dropped out of college. She had tried to commit suicide, but the attempt failed. Now the guy was asking her to run away with him. I waited as she spilled her story. "What should I do?" she asked.

I asked her questions: What are your plans for college? Before you met this guy, what were your plans for the future?

If you were on the outside looking in and a friend came to you with this story, what would you tell her? By the end of our phone call, she had found the answers, and none of them had come from me; she knew the right thing to do. Before we hung up, I asked if I could pray with her. At this point she was ready. Had I tried to lecture her on the recklessness of her decisions, she never would have discovered the answers for herself.

Her past decisions *were* irresponsible, and she had made a mess of her life. She already knew that. That's why she called for help. She needed to figure out how to get out of the quagmire in which she found herself. If I had jumped in with a spiritual or moral lesson in the beginning, I might not have reached her. I would not have had the opportunity to pray with her and hear her say how much she needed God. Our conversation was a journey, one in which we worked together so that she could see the situation clearly. My part was to listen as she found her way.

When your teen does open up, some of the things he tells you might shock you or frighten you. How do you react when your "baby" lets you in on the scary details of her world? Let's look at the next reason teens don't talk to their parents.

REASON #3—MY PARENTS WOULD FREAK OUT

I am careful what I tell my parents. My mom is very sensitive. There are some things that she would not want to hear. I tell my dad more things because he can handle more, but he still prefers for me to keep things that are shocking to myself.

Michelle H., age 17

Some teens protect their parents because they know that their moms or dads will consider the reality too unsettling. God is relevant in today's society. He's not afraid of tough issues, nor should we be. We have to toughen up so we can point our teens to a God who will walk with them no matter what they encounter. We have to learn to listen first and freak out later, because teens that protect their parents from the scary details carry their burdens alone. Worse, they are forced to make critical decisions unaided.

I hide the reality of my world because they can't do anything about it.

Linda S., age 14

Too many teens try to make their way alone. Much like a coach in a football game, our teens are in the game of life, and we are on the sidelines. They experience victories and defeats on their own, but every once in a while they signal for a time-out. Though we can't fix everything for them, we can let them know that we're available to help. We can offer to come up with new plays to help them get the ball across the finish line.

When teens share the gruesome details of their experiences, their intent is not to frighten or shock us. They may feel overwhelmed, or they may be looking for encouragement. When my daughter entered her freshman year of college, she shared with me some problems that her friends were facing. What she told me was disquieting, but she was asking me to pray for her friends because she loved them. She wasn't asking me to put a high wall around her to protect her. She simply needed support.

The one thing that my parents do to impact my faith is to be fully supportive...to listen, that's the most important thing.

Vicki M., age 21

Sadly, there was a time when my daughter wouldn't have come to me because I made it almost impossible for her to do so. Is it okay if I'm honest with you? I knew teens, and yet I panicked when it came to my own kids. My children had proved that they were trustworthy, but when I saw other youth making poor decisions, I pulled in the reins. I became stricter at a time when my teens' actions were demonstrating that it was time for me to trust them. This nailed shut any attempts at real communication. My kids weren't going to tell me what was going on in their world. Why would they if they were forced to suffer the consequences for things they weren't doing? The price tag was simply too high.

After a few months, I realized our relationships had taken a downturn because we were no longer talking about things that mattered. I felt as if I were standing outside a door marked with a huge "X." I was on one side of the door, and my teens were on the other. This is what my daughter had to say about that period of our lives:

I think the whole "I trust you but I don't trust who you are with" is legitimate. I just think that when that is used, the parent automatically takes herself out of a major portion of her child's life. If you truly know your child and know that her friends won't sway her, then that rule should be kicked to the curb. If it is, your child won't be afraid to tell you everything. The only difference between parents who trust their child in the world he lives in and parents who are scared for their children is that the scared parents don't know what is going on.

Melissa E., age 19

What is your teen trying to tell you? Is he looking for your help or advice? Is she asking you to pray for her and encourage her? What is your reaction to the things you hear from him? If you freak out when he shares something with you, you might as well put a sign on your forehead that says, "No Vacancies," because the chances of your teen coming back are slim.

REASON #4—MY PARENTS WILL TRY TO FIX IT

As I wrote this I realized how much I love my parents, despite their faults, and how much they love me, despite mine. And how much they must be like God, watching us, letting us screw up, but loving us with such a deep, abiding, everlasting love that we will never comprehend it.

Karianne P., age 17

Question: Would you tell your parents if you made a terrible mistake?

Hundreds of teens responded to the above question with, "It depends." After probing further, I discovered that if a mistake or a problem were so obvious that the teens' parents would eventually find out, the teens would talk to them about it. If it was huge, like a pregnancy or an addiction, they wanted their parents' help. But if the mistake or problem was minor or less than earth shattering, they wanted to handle it themselves. It wasn't a matter of trying to hide the mistake, but rather wanting to work through the problem on their own.

During my son's first year of college, he let some important things slide. He did well in many areas but struggled in others. When he shared the news with us, our impulse was to get him back on track. My husband and I discussed our plan. As we talked, I thought about the stacks of surveys sitting in my home office that were about this very topic. Ryan wasn't looking for us to fix the problem but to be there for him while he fixed it himself. We let him know that we recognized the positive things he had accomplished and that we would trust him to take care of the rest. It wasn't easy. He went on to make some decisions that we might not have, but later we saw the results. He assumed total responsibility for his choices. He might not have done it the way we would have, but he owned the decisions he made and the resulting successes. It was a real step of maturity on his part, and I was proud of him. There comes a point when we have to allow our children the luxury of making mistakes and learning to work through them.

Question: What would you hope your parents would do if you made a mistake?

It depends upon the situation. If I were older, I would want their support and forgiveness, but not necessarily their help. I would want to do it myself and be the adult I was brought up to be.

Teddi H., age 13

Teens have definite ideas on how they want a parent to

help when they mess up. Their suggestions included forgiveness, encouragement, and pointing them in the right direction. Teens define help as encouragement, not as parents jumping in to fix the problem. They aren't looking for instant solutions but for someone to show them how to learn from their mistakes.

I know that they would be disappointed, but I hope in a "let's see how we can make this better" kind of way.

Rebecca C., age 17

If you want to fix your teen's mistakes or problems, you're not alone. It's instinct. Our teens were once innocent babies and we protected them. We put locks on the cabinets so they wouldn't drink Drano®. We kissed the bruises on their knees when they fell down. We taught them how to look both ways before crossing the street. We represented total authority and protection in their lives.

As parents of teens, our role has changed. We don't abdicate our responsibilities simply because our teens' voices have changed, but we do have to recognize that our teens will face difficult times. Sometimes they will make blunders, and blunders are growth opportunities. How we react will determine the amount of maturity our teens gain from the experience. If we try to make all of their problems go away or protect them from learning from their mistakes, we stunt their growth.

When we moved here it was real hard. Then I had some other things happen, and that was hard on me, but my mom taught me that God doesn't just walk away and leave you hanging. He's got something better waiting for me.

Laura N., age 15

Reason #5—My Parents Don't Know Who I Am

Just because my older sister made some bad mistakes in life, don't think it's your [the parents'] fault. Stop thinking that way. I'm not like her; so don't always deny me because you think I'll make the same judgments in my life.

Kim Z., age 18

Sometimes teens will not approach their parents because they feel defeated before they ever start. This happens when parents make decisions that have nothing to do with the character of an individual teen or the actual situation. An example of this is when rules for one child are based upon the actions of another sibling.

This is what I would say to my mom if I could say just one thing: I am not you. I am not my sister. Therefore I cannot be like you or her. I have my own way of doing things, and all things change with time. It is no longer 1974 or 1992. I am my own person.

Carrie R., age 17

Teens also feel defeated when we force consequences for our own mistakes upon our children. I met Lara when she was fifteen years old. Today she is a senior in high school. She's an amazing young woman, though she's not had it easy in life. Her mom married young, and her dad left when she was about ten years old. Her mother tried to do the best she could for her children, but the men who came in and out of her life through marriage and divorce made Lara's home life unstable and at times unbearable. They lived in near poverty at times, and they moved often.

Lara started attending church and accepted Christ as her Savior. This changed her entire world. She grew in her love for God. She became a leader in the Christian group that met after school. Her outgoing personality and faith encouraged others in her youth group. Soon after Lara was saved, her mom began to attend church and made a commitment of faith.

This should have been a wonderful event for the entire family, but it wasn't. Lara's mother realized how her past decisions had affected her family. She zeroed in on her children, watching their every move to protect them from falling into the same traps she had. Her parenting decisions had nothing to do with her children's character but everything to do with her own mistakes. Her friends had caused disaster in her life, so she forbade Lara to hang out with anyone who was not a Christian. What she didn't understand was that Lara was a positive influence on others. Lara invited her friends to church and to the Teens for Christ group at school. She was respected for her faith and her friendliness, but now she could no longer even eat lunch with her unsaved friends at school.

I know what is right and wrong. They instilled it in me when I was young, and now it's time for me to actually live it, but they won't let me, so I don't tell them everything so I can live it out. In all honesty, I want to do what is right, and I aim to do it. Part of growing up is making mistakes along the way and learning from them.

Beth, age 17

Lara's mom started regulating her daughter's Bible reading times and checked to make sure her daughter was listening to Christian music. Though her motivation was pure, she was frustrating her daughter. Lara struggled as her faith became less about a relationship with God and more about keeping her mom appeased. She was living under rules that had nothing to do with her. She stopped talking to her mom about her life because everything she told her mom could be used as ammunition for making new rules. Though Lara's mom did not intentionally set out to discourage her daughter, Lara gave up and stopped attending church. It was simply too hard to live her faith by her mother's standards.

A critical part of parenting is to understand who your teens are and where they are spiritually and emotionally—and to make choices based on that information.

My parents have always been very aware of what is going on with kids my age. I think that some parents choose not to know what their teens are being exposed to, but my parents were secure enough with me to know that I am not a product of my environment.

Rachel K., age 18

What About My Teen?

There are so many opportunities to do bad, immoral things. For example, I go to bars and get drunk. I would never tell my parents any of this!

Samantha W., age 19

What about the teens who are not talking because they are making destructive life choices and don't want us to know? I would be naïve to ignore the fact that many parents feel as if they have no answers. As a youth worker, I have lain on my face before God and wept over the teens who have walked away from God. I have sat beside teens in our youth meetings who hate everything about church and who only come because they are forced to attend. I have had teens avoid me in public because they are doing things that they would be embarrassed for me to see.

There are parents who have spent hours praying for their teens. These parents feel as if the heavens have closed and God cannot, or is not, hearing their prayers. You may have picked up this book because your teen is not trustworthy. Some of you may wonder where your child has gone and who the angry, disruptive teen is that has taken his or her place. There are parents reading this book who have made mistakes with their teens and desperately want a second chance. You may be hurting over the broken relationship between you and your child. I pray that the information in this book will be a tool in the process of healing. I encourage you to decide right now that you will not give up. If I've learned one thing from ministering to teens, it is that teens need someone to continue to believe in them even when they don't believe in themselves.

Sometimes we need to place our loved ones in God's hands as we work on the only people we can really change—ourselves. Refocus your sights on the relationship between you and your teen, rather than on the problems. This is similar to an old house we once owned. Unsightly cracks zigzagged across the ceiling, and we tried several times to patch them. Within weeks they would reappear. We called in a specialist to help us fix the ceiling. He took one look and then pointed at the floor. "It's not a ceiling problem. It's a foundation problem. I could put in a brand new ceiling and within a year you'd have the same problem." Sometimes it's the same way with our teens. We focus on them and point out the cracks and flaws, thinking that if we could fix our teens everything would be perfect once again. Yet if we can work on the foundation—our relationships with our teens—then hopefully repairs to the relationships will last. Listening is a key factor to beginning that process.

As you read through the following chapters, I hope that something a teen says will give you insight that will help you take the next step. You are important to your teen—even if he isn't showing it right now. Restoring your relationship with your teen takes time, but the rewards make it worthwhile.

A Price to Pay

Teens need constant and unconditional love from parents. With a few basic skills—like working on communication—they will portray that love, and everything else will fall into place.

Travis R., age 18

Learning to listen is not easy. Listening is a learned behavior, and it will cost you something. For some of you it will be hard to bite your tongues as you listen to what your teens are saying. For others, you might get discouraged when your teens reject you in the beginning. Your teens might distrust your motives until they see that you are really reaching out. Some teens might tell their parents what they think their parents want to hear. If your teen clams up, your instinct will be to throw up your hands in frustration—but don't give up! Breaking the silence between you and your child will not happen overnight.

Becoming a good listener is a process, but one that offers the reward of a stronger relationship between you and your teen.

Make It Real

Ask God for Help

Start praying for the foundation of your relationship to be made whole today. Even if your relationship is close, ask God to help you carry part of your teen's burden.

Ask God to toughen you up and to help you learn to listen first and freak out later.

Begin to pray for your teen on a daily basis. Pray that God will guide and protect him or her.

Ask God to begin to develop his plan in the life of your teen.

Ask God to change anything in you that needs to be changed in order to take your relationship with your teen to the next level. Praise God for your teen and the destiny he has for his or her life.

Anticipate what God is going to do in your relationship with your teen.

Let's Talk

Make a date with your teen. Take her to a quiet place where you can have lunch or dinner, or go to a park. Let your teen know (in as few words as possible) that you want to listen to what she has to say. Tell her that your relationship with her is important to you. Ask her if there is anything that you do that frustrates her or pushes her away. Assure her that you will listen and not be offended or respond with advice or lectures. Then do just that.

Don't push beyond this point. Don't try to delve deeper. At this point, you simply want to show your teen that you are open to hearing what she has to say. Your teen may say something that wounds you, and your instinct will be to make it personal. Remember that the point of this is to fix the foundation and to learn to listen. She may be right, or she may be totally wrong, but listen for the heartbeat behind her words instead of trying to defend yourself.

Your teen might show you a different perspective. She might even share some real issues in her life. Let your teen know that you care, that you'll be praying for her, and that you're available if she needs you for advice. Even if she doesn't respond (don't push it if she doesn't), this exercise might open the door a crack when she realizes that you really do want to listen.

A couple of reminders:

(1) I didn't promise it would be easy.

(2) Trust develops over time.

Chapter Two

Reality Check

We must adjust to changing times
and still hold to unchanging principles.

—James Earl "Jimmy" Carter Jr.
39th U.S. President

Question: Many parents feel as if they understand what teens go through because they were once teens. Do you believe that?

Yes, our parents have gone through teenage life, but they haven't gone through our life. There's a big difference. We all grow up and mature, but in different ways depending upon the things that influence us. The advice that they give is based upon what they went through, not from our lifestyle.

Janelle T., age 15

"TIME KEEPS ON SLIPPING, SLIPPING, SLIPPING INTO THE FUTURE ..."

If you recognize the above lyrics as part of a song titled "Fly Like an Eagle," you are most likely a child of the late seventies. Though those years might seem like the Stone Age to our teens, most parents recall the issues that came with being a teenager in those days. There were drugs and alcohol and sexual pressure, even way back then. Teens had fights behind the school and at football games. There were dysfunctional families in our neighborhoods. We faced issues of self-esteem, and body image was key to relationships and popularity. We had pimples and bemoaned being too short, too tall, too fat, or too thin. There were bullies and cruel teenagers who made life miserable for the less fortunate—whether that was due to money, looks, or popularity. I can still tell you the name of the guy who said he liked my personality but would only date me if I had a bag over my head...but I digress. There were cliques. There was peer pressure. All of these were challenges that shaped us. The memories may be distant, but they are distinct. Then why is it so difficult to share our experiences with our teens, and why can't they relate to our war stories of what it was like to be a teenager in the seventies? It's because time has truly slipped, slipped, slipped away into the future.

Parents were kids once too. I don't think they forget what it was like, but they forget that times have changed. I think that is a huge deterrent in effective communication between teens and their parents.

Sarah H., age 15

The reality is that even though you and I faced many of the same issues, being a teenager is different for our kids than it was for us, because our frame of reference is different. Though we have all been teenagers, we as parents have never been teenagers in today's society.

When we say to our teens, "I was a teen once," they take it with a grain of salt. It's like a fifty-five-year-old woman sharing advice on pregnancy and birthing with a twenty-five-year-old mother-to-be. The basics are the same. There is no doubt as to the experience and wisdom behind the older woman's words. But there have been tremendous changes in the past thirty years. It's not that one line of thinking or experience is right and the other is wrong. They're simply different because the time frame is different. The advice of the older woman is valuable, but the mother-to-be weighs it in light of the changes that have taken place since the days when the older woman was having children.

Back in their day it was not "cool" to have sex, and now it is almost expected. Certain things have changed. Teenagers have always had the same feelings and confusion and hardships as they do now. We are just in a different time.

Michelle H., age 17

It's no different with parents and teens today. Though many of the issues that surround your teens are the same as what you once encountered, there have been significant cultural changes that have made these issues more complex. Let's take a look at how things have developed and how that impacts your teenagers.

Sex

Question: More than any other generation, the boundaries have fallen away in the area of sex for your generation. How does that affect you?

To me, it seems the youth are more open to a free-for-all sex culture. Kim R., age 19

My daughter recently challenged me to listen to a teen radio station. "If you really want to know what teens are saying about sex, listen to the after-midnight broadcast," she said. I tuned in and was not only surprised; I was angry. The radio hosts discussed every type of sexual act with their teen audience. They chatted with teens of all ages as they delved into topics including homosexuality, group sex, oral sex, and other issues. No topic was taboo. This program twisted the moral viewpoint of thousands of teens while parents had no idea that sex was being introduced in a way that might be objectionable to them. Though this radio program shook me, it is not news to millions of teens. This generation has truly heard it all.

Once, one of my teens said something about sex in a joking manner, and it stopped me in my tracks. I've always been very open with my teens about sex, and it's not a difficult subject at all for me to broach, but this was something extremely intimate about the sexual act itself.

"How do you know about that?" I asked.

My teen laughed. "Mom, I hear that kind of stuff around the lunch table. Are you kidding me?"

Youth are much more sexually active these days, but I hear a lot of youth my age say that it has always been this way. It's just that people are more open about it now. I still strongly believe that God made sex to be between a man and a woman and for those two to be married before being intimate. People who are okay with sex before marriage and with [having sex with] tons of people go through many different relationships and don't have as strong a foundation in life. Those that don't believe in sex before marriage are completely the opposite. They look for more God-glorifying relationships rather than relations to serve their own wants and needs.

Jen W., age 15

Sometimes we mistakenly believe that because our children attend church or have relationships with God they are in some way sheltered from sexual pressure or from the influence of the new sexual norms. The truth is that most teens—even those who choose not to have sex until marriage—are shaped by a culture bombarded with sexual messages. They don't have to listen to a radio show. They hear about it at school, among their friends, in chat rooms on the Internet, in music, on television, and even in their favorite catalogs and commercials.

Sex Sells

Sex is not as meaningful anymore to most people. It makes it harder for those of us who want it to be, because it's everywhere, and it's harder to stay mentally pure.

Jessica M., age 16

We live in a culture that is sexually saturated. In our American society sex sells beer, cars, clothing, and even shampoo. Advertising dollars are aimed directly at your teens. Ad executives have discovered that if a young consumer believes that a product will make him more desirable to the opposite sex, he'll buy it, even if it is only a product for hair care. They know that teens will spend money in their stores if the message fits into their definition of image. Our teens are targeted because youth have incredible consumer power. Go to the mall on a Saturday and check the age of the average shopper. You will discover a mass of teens buying cosmetics, clothes, music, and accessories.

One popular store that sells clothing to teens distributes a catalog with graphic nude and sexual images that are labeled as pornographic by many parents and watchdog organizations. Out of 250 pages in a recent catalog, only 100 of the pages were clothing ads. The rest included articles with tongue-in-cheek advice and graphic articles on dating and sex. Photographs of teens, alone and in groups, were featured in a mixture of erotic poses and various stages of nudity. Many of our teens are desensitized to this because they are bombarded with similar messages.

From radio to sitcoms to movies to music, sex is an underlying message. How does this affect your teen? The cultural definition of sex is introduced at such a young age and is so pervasive that our teens struggle with the concept of the sanctity of sex. Advertisements are cleverly written and, for the most part, teens (and adults) miss the underlying messages, though the influence ads have upon our teens and on society is strong. We are barraged with a host of messages, and our filtering system has shut down.

It affects youth in families in our secular culture because there are no lines and nothing is sacred anymore.

Helen V., age 16

Sex and the Media

I know tons of people who have believed the sex lies sold to them by the media. It made me somewhat like that before I was saved. I wanted to be accepted, and I tried to make myself like [the same as] my friends. This really affects teens. To be different and possess different values means less friends and acceptance.

Sarah C., age 19

How has the media changed since you were a teen? I recently watched a television program that several of the teens in our home church love to watch. The main character had sex with a girl he had just met. The sex was casual, kind of like when two friends have a good talk—except it wasn't two friends and it definitely wasn't casual. This is the entertainment world of our youth's culture—both churched and unchurched teens.

Why would Christian teens not only watch these types of shows, but also consider them among their favorites? It's because sex is not considered a big deal. They see it and hear about it so much that they feel that they will make their decisions independent of these types of influences.

Sex is definitely more casual and not such a big deal anymore. Purity isn't really shown as something to be taken seriously. However, I can make choices on my own. I can see that what movies show isn't always right. I've been taught better than that.

April W., age 14

But what about the teens who are not offered a balance to the media messages? Though I talk all the time with teens who, like April, have made conscious decisions not to have sex until they are married, I also meet teens like Katie.

What is portrayed (in the media) is not true. Once you do it, there is no way to go back.

Ben N., age 17

Katie and I were talking as I walked to my car after a service. "Does sex really count if you just hook up for five minutes in the back seat of a car?" she asked. For the next half-hour, Katie and I visited as she shared the details surrounding her question.

Katie was smart and pretty. She was fifteen and the type of Christian teen that I meet much more often now: nonreligious, newly in love with God, but with a significant history shaped by her home life or cultural norms. She already had experienced a considerable number of sexual encounters and openly shared that fact from the beginning. I'll never forget her look of confusion as she attempted to explain what had happened. "I know that I'm supposed to stay away from sex before marriage, but this was no big deal," she said. "It didn't mean anything to me. I'm not sure if I'll ever even see this guy again. If it didn't mean anything to either of us, I'm not sure why should it mean something to God."

I tried to put it into context. "Katie, when God is your dancing partner, he doesn't like anybody else cutting in," I said. I shared how valuable she was to God and why sex is reserved for a lifetime commitment. I wanted her to comprehend that she was worth more than a five-minute hookup in the back of a car. As we talked further, I saw a look of understanding flood Katie's face. The truth is that Katie struggled with this issue because there was nothing in her upbringing that said that casual sex is harmful or wrong. It takes time to completely change a person's way of thinking, but Katie is definitely open to God working in this area of her life.

The biggest problem facing teens is the media influence on teens. The peer pressure that comes from media (especially television) is phenomenal.

Eleanor T., age 16

The message Katie received in her past was that sex is exciting and fun and that everybody is doing it. Ministering to teens like her not only means sharing that premarital sex is wrong but also sending a clear message that sex is a gift from God and that there are boundaries in place because God wants the best for each of us. A huge part of any youth ministry has become helping teens grasp something other than the cultural definition of love, which is "easy sex without long-term commitment."

It's a shame how sex has become just a fun thing to do. It's supposed to be a sacred thing between a man and a woman. I wear a True Love Waits ring to remind me of that. I want to remain pure for my future spouse, because I know that is the best thing for everyone and it is what God wants from me. God knows what he's talking about. After all, he created sex.

Sarah H., age 15

ERODING BOUNDARIES

If any topic is championed long enough, it loses its edge. Once it loses its edge, it becomes commonplace. Once it's commonplace, it becomes normal. That is what has happened in our society in many areas. Though our nation is comprised of a very small percentage of homosexuals, gays have a significant voice in our culture. Nudging homosexuality into broader areas such as the media made it commonplace. For many teens, homosexuality is such a mainstream topic that it has become a cultural norm. When boundaries are pushed to the edge, a clear message is sent that everything goes—yet it fails to show the consequences and the lasting harm a lack of boundaries inflicts on both families and individuals.

The boundaries changing for our culture has affected teens a lot. Most kids around go for "quantity" rather than "quality."

Ricky M., age 16

Teen movies depict a generation out of control—like a giant fraternity party pulled along by hormonal strings—yet adults are the ones who make the vast majority of these films. These filmmakers do teens no favors by stereotyping them. They fail to represent the thousands of teens who are making decisions to stay faithful to remaining abstinent until marriage.

All of these things seriously downplay the beauty of sex in a marriage. I was once told by a guy that waiting for sex is stupid, that it isn't that big of a deal. He apparently forgot that it is a big deal. God designed sex to belong in a marriage. I still have that belief, but it is hard to maintain that. It's not just the sex issue, but also the fact that it is pushed so far. That in itself puts down the value of sex.

Meredith G., age 17

When movies romanticize or downplay sex and leave out the message of lifetime commitment, they offer a confusing message to a generation hungering for relationships. Unfortunately, too many teens buy into that message until they realize that the one-dimensional picture of love, sex, and romance that they've seen in the media failed to tell the whole story.

THE PRICE TAG—STDs AND PREGNANCY

The biggest thing that has changed since you were a teen is that sex carries a heavier price tag than just unwed pregnancy. Up to twenty-nine percent of sexually active adolescent girls have been infected with chlamydia. In a single act of unprotected sex with an infected partner, a teenage woman has a one percent risk of acquiring HIV, a thirty percent risk of getting genital herpes, and a fifty percent chance of contracting gonorrhea. One in four sexually experienced teens acquires an STD. These statistics reflect diseases that can last a lifetime or even end a life prematurely.[1]

I heard a statistic a couple of months ago that said that about fifty percent of graduating seniors are not virgins, and those statistics aren't much different for Christians. This makes me sad! Everywhere I look, youth are making horrible decisions to have sex before marriage, and then they suffer the consequences. Even if I weren't a Christian I would want to remain a virgin.

Lanae P., age 19

The rate of teenage STDs is up, but pregnancy rates are dropping. A study released in April 2003 by the Physicians Consortium concluded that there has been a sixty-seven percent drop in pregnancy rates in unmarried girls due to abstinence.[2] However, there are still almost one million teenage girls—eleven percent of all teens aged fifteen to nineteen and twenty-two percent of those who have had sexual intercourse—who become pregnant each year.

It breaks my heart, because I see these girls with babies when they are (in my eyes) still babies themselves.

Jennifer T., age 19

Seventeen-year-old Heather is one of them. When I interviewed her, her baby was due any day. Life as she'd known it had come to a halt. It was her senior year of high school. All of her future plans, as well as her image of love, had been restructured to fit her present reality of being a mom. She responded to my survey, and this is what she had to say:

I fell for the whole "I love you and we'll be together forever" bit myself. Parents need to start talking to their kids about it [sex] early, so they don't follow in the world's footsteps.

Heather Y., age 17

ABORTION

Abortion statistics are also declining. One survey by Zogby International[3] says the pro-life shift seems to be most pronounced among younger Americans, with one-third of those ages eighteen to twenty-nine saying that abortion should never be legal. That contrasts with about twenty-three percent for those ages thirty to sixty-four.

The Bible states that God knows you even in your mother's womb, so abortion is a big deal. Having an abortion is taking away the life that God created.

Meredith G., age 17

Though abortion rates are declining, the aftereffects of abortion are widespread as teens and young women come to grips with the reality of their decisions. A couple of years ago I talked with a teen who had been quiet at youth events for several weeks—a red flag for this friendly, outgoing girl. When I asked what was wrong, she broke down and told me that she had had an abortion. The enormity of what she had lost overwhelmed her. She loved God, but she had made a huge mistake. She attended a party, started drinking, and lost her virginity that night. She knew that neither she nor the baby's father was prepared to be a parent. She didn't love him. They were mere acquaintances, and she hadn't seen him since that night. A couple of her friends at school confided that they had had abortions and recommended a clinic. There she was told that her abortion would be a painless and easy procedure. They described it in terms such as "emptying the contents" and "D and C."

The clinic failed to explain how she would feel the next day. "They didn't tell me that I would wake up hating myself," she said. We wept together as she asked God to step in and help her heal. There was nothing I could do to take away her pain. There were no words that could bring the baby back. All I could do was love her and direct her to a God who could put her back together.

I went with a friend. It's a lot more than what the doctors say.

Seriously, it was the most horrific experience for my friend. She still has back flashes from the experience.

Beth, age 17

No one wants to hear that a Christian teen has experienced an abortion. Avoiding abortions is one reason we teach our teens about the beauty of sex within marriage. It's one reason we tell them how to make choices that will not only keep them sexually pure but also help them find the intimacy they desire in a relationship with God.

I am thankful that this teen was honest with me, because most carry the burden alone. It is a solitary place to walk when a teen feels as if she is the only one who feels guilt, remorse, shame, and emotional pain. Our teens are torn between their belief system and the cultural stand that abortion is a choice and that the baby is only a fetus. There are thousands of teens who silently deal with the emotional aftermath of an abortion when they realize that they have been told a lie.

Many teens have tried to make this true (sex without consequences), but only ended up getting themselves into huge messes, emotional wrecks, and finding that they have wasted quality time on something that falsely claimed to have fulfillment.

Keith J., age 21

One of the reasons teens are having fewer abortions is that they are waking up to the reality of abortion and they are angry. It is their generation that has paid the price as millions of their peers never made it out of the womb. Teens are expressing strong views on abortion, as confirmed in the passionate wording that they used when responding to my survey.

Out of the hundreds of teens interviewed, only two felt abortion was a viable option. Several teens referred me to Web sites that demonstrated different abortion procedures. The mix of Christian teens who responded were from both Christian and non-Christian homes. They were all ages. They were from all over the country. Many had friends who had had an abortion. All of them said that abortion, whether they had experienced it or not, whether they supported it or not, was definitely a "big deal." Many teens expressed compassion for those of their own generation who had experienced abortion.

If I was pregnant out of wedlock and felt like the world was over for me, I would be vulnerable, and I might not completely understand what a beautiful blessing is inside of me.

Anna A., age 15

Oral Sex

The biggest problem facing teens is sex and intimacy before its time. Parents can help by being open and honest, actually talking to their kids and knowing what's going on ...

Helen V., age 16

For many of you, just the introduction of this topic makes you uncomfortable. *"You're going to talk about that?"* It's important that we discuss it because this is something that is a real part of your teen's sexual culture.

It changes the definition of sex; there is controversy on what actually is sex.

Becky S., age 18

Oral sex is not considered sex among the overall youth culture. Many teens see this as an option to experience sex while, in their minds, still remaining abstinent. Additionally, many teens consider oral sex to be a no-risk sexual act. They do not realize the number of documented sexually transmitted diseases that are transmitted through oral sex including herpes, syphilis, gonorrhea, genital warts (HPV), and hepatitis A. We may want to attribute this problem and the new attitude among youth to a past president, but the real conversation we should be having is what impact this has on our teens and preteens.

No physical or emotional consequences? Who fed us that lie? I don't believe that to be true in my world at all. Once you give your virginity away to someone, it hurts like no other. It's a gift that you can give only once. It will cause you physical and emotional pain. You might become depressed, or rumors might go around saying you are "easy." You could end up with an irreversible STD. That alone could cause not only physical pain, but emotional pain and sorrow. The media feeds us as teens a bunch of stupidity. Save it for that one special person.

Adam D., age 18

Oral sex happens during the lunch hour at school, at parties, at football games, at home, and in cars. I interviewed a nineteen-year-old college sophomore who shared his story. He started having oral sex in high school, as did many of his friends. He felt that it was harmless since no one could get pregnant and it involved little or no emotional attachment. As time progressed, his behavior became riskier. Many of his encounters were with complete strangers. He was handsome, well liked, respected, and girls were flattered by the initial attention he gave them, though he barely remembered their names after the encounters. At college, he met a Christian girl and they began to date. He kept his sexual life a secret from her. One day he made a phone call to a friend to brag about a girl he had met on a bus. He talked in detail about what had occurred. He accidentally hit the record button on his cell phone, and later that conversation showed up as a message. When he listened to it, he heard his own voice telling the grisly details.

Hearing that message was a harsh moment of truth. He listened to the guy bragging on the phone—the one who was hurting his girlfriend and using girls to attain a sexual high. He heard clearly the sexual addiction, the selfishness, and the lows he had attained in pursuit of conquests. He was overwhelmed and sat on the curb. When a friend came by, he stopped to ask what was wrong. "I'm trapped and I hate myself," he said. He let his friend listen to the message. "That's who I have become," he said. His friend was a Christian and explained how to ask for God's forgiveness and offered accountability.

Today that young man is serving God. He and his girlfriend plan to marry after college. He continues to be accountable to a group of Christian men. It was uncomfortable for him to share his story, but he wanted parents to understand that oral sex is a trap that many teens fall into and that it is real. He realizes how strong the battle is, because it was a long and hard process for him to change. He had to come clean with his girlfriend. He had to be honest with God. He wants adults to understand that sexual addiction is a rising phenomenon among youth.

This teen's story is not unique. A recent survey reported

that fifty-five percent of teens aged thirteen to nineteen admitted to engaging in oral sex.[4] In a small suburban area of Colorado, parents were distressed by an article featured in the high school paper. A student cited a survey that reported that sixty percent of the student body did not consider oral sex to be a sexual act. It further reported that forty percent of the 274 students surveyed had experienced oral sex and did so to receive satisfaction without losing their innocence or respect. The author, a student, went on to describe the act in graphic terms. The intent of the article was to reveal that oral sex was unsafe. While it might not have had a huge impact on the teens, it was a wake-up call for the parents in the small community. Though oral sex is a difficult topic to discuss, especially for adults, it's a trend that all parents should note.

In spite of the fact that thousands of Christian teens choose to abstain from sexual intercourse and all other forms of sex, oral sex and sexual addictions are issues that affect many relationships. It is difficult for a generation that perceives oral sex as simply a sexual high or release to trust in relationships based upon sacrificial love and commitment, especially when sex carries no emotional significance. This trend not only affects our youth today, but also has the potential to affect future relationships and family bonds.

ALTERNATIVE SEXUAL LIFESTYLES

Question: If you take a stand on issues such as homosexuality, do you pay a price for taking that stand?

People have so many views today. It's normal for everyone to have a different opinion.

Jessica M., age 16

You might not be cool with homosexuality, but this generation is. Your teens are introduced to alternative sexual lifestyles at a very young age. I recently visited with an older gay man. He said, "When I was a teen and struggling with my sexual identity, it was much harder. After all, we didn't have *Will and Grace*." The power of the media can never be underestimated. Television shows depicting witty, beautiful, charming gay teens or adults impact our culture. The fact is that there are attractive, clever, and talented gay people in our world, in our neighborhood, and in our church. We just don't see them because we choose not to.

Many teens struggle with why we do not embrace—or at least welcome—this lifestyle and the people involved. Two things can occur. One, adults fail to realize that teens have been raised within their culture to condone homosexuality and we falsely assume that they will share our convictions. And two, the way the local church and Christians react to homosexuals can create barriers.

Teens are looking for unconditional love. They measure our commitment to a faith built on love by our response to the homosexual community. Though homosexuality may seem faceless to an older generation, homosexuals have both a face *and* a name to youth. The concept of homosexuality as a lifestyle choice has been a part of their culture since they were born. Remember, their life span is less than two decades. Much of what has happened in the gay community occurred as they grew up and formulated their opinions.

I'm not sure of my thoughts on homosexuality. I accept it, but I know that God says that a man shouldn't lay down with another man. However, God also says things about divorce that have changed now.

Louise C., age 16

Louise's statement is powerful because it reflects a question asked not only by teens, but also by unbelievers. What are our Christian convictions, and why are some things acceptable and others not? Why is homosexuality a sin and divorce condoned? Issues such as these confuse teens attempting to know the truth.

You are looked upon as a bigot or an ignorant person. This is when you have to turn to Jesus for strength and guidance.

Jeremy K., age 18

When Christian teens do take a stand against homosexuality as a practice, they most likely will be branded as bigots or labeled intolerant. Teens who hold convictions on this and many other issues fight a battle that most adults don't even understand. They have to choose between what a nation perceives as a norm and what the Bible deems sin. They do this with the understanding that their convictions will not be appreciated or understood by many of their friends and acquaintances.

I've been called closed-minded and bigoted for not accepting those decisions as okay. It seems to me that people get very defensive when I say something as non-confrontational as "I disagree with you." Standing up for your convictions has become pretty unpopular.

Amanda B., age 18

How do our teens deal with believing homosexuality is sin in a culture that does not? Our teens try to reach out to homosexuals through compassionate ministry. Most teens see homosexuality as only one of many sins that Jesus came to redeem. They see the homosexual as a person—a possible seeker—just as Jesus did. Like Christ, they see the sin, but not in any different light than any other sin. They reach out in ways their parents might not have felt comfortable doing, allowing them to share the news of hope because they see the person and not the sin. In this area of ministry and others, teens have much to teach the church and Christian adults. They minister to the homosexual in the same way Jesus reached out to the woman at the well, with a message of love, worth, and redemption.

A wedge can be driven between you and someone close to you due to the fact that you take a different standpoint. In the case of homosexuality, you might be labeled. However, I believe that you should love the homosexual and hate the sin.

Carrie R., age 18

THE GOOD NEWS ABOUT SEX!

I know it [sex outside of marriage] is wrong, and I do not agree with any of that. I don't watch it, and I don't take it in. I'm a virgin and will stay so until I'm married.

Melissa A., age 18

Are you ready for some good news? I can see parents all

across the nation taking a deep breath. "Good news?" you ask. "Bring it on!"

Every teen is not having wild sex. Many desire stability and are searching for real answers concerning how to remain abstinent and form lasting relationships. Barna Research Group reported that eighty-two percent of today's teens desire to have one marriage partner for life.[5] Mosaic teens (born after 1984) are curving back to embrace more traditional ideas about sex. These views contradict even those of their peers from just ten years ago.

I have always understood the importance of sex in marriage only and that having sex outside of marriage is something that we are not ready for.

Steven S., age 16

Mosaic teens understand the consequences of casual sex because they are living with those consequences. If they are not experiencing the consequences, they see those who are. They question those who promise sex without commitment or boundaries.

Teens are hungry for more than just physical intimacy, and they are finding out that sex and drugs do not satisfy, because it's not real love. It's empty and leaves you with heartache and misery. A turn is coming around the corner with a new standard. As far as the media goes, all of my friends have taken a stand against it. We are not supporting organizations or going to see movies that support pornography. Many teens want to get into the movie, film, and business world in hopes of changing the tides.

Michelle H., age 17

Some teens have more conservative views than their

parents do. In fact, this is a growing trend that I see across the nation when I speak with teens. These are youth caught in the middle. They have to stand against the trends in their own culture as well as defend their belief system to their parents.

When my old (first and only) boyfriend broke up with me after eleven months, I cried a lot and was really depressed, and I didn't want to talk about it. My mom thought that I was pregnant and was totally okay with that. I don't know how I feel about that. Having her be okay with me being pregnant is really weird. That made matters worse. I couldn't believe that my mom thought I would have sex! So that has changed, as in I think that it is wrong and she is still confused about it all.

Brianna B., age 16

Many teens have come to the decision that premarital sex is wrong after the painful realization that easy sex is costly. Teens around our nation have decided that they will take a stand and that there is another way—even if their parents don't go along for the ride.

Sex is one of the biggest problems teens face. Some parents condone premarital sex ... saying it's all right. Parents need to be supportive of the fact that premarital sex is wrong, not right. I think a lot of teens might not have as much trouble in their lives if their parents were good influences.

Elizabeth H., age 14

While our natural inclination might be to avoid talking with our teens about sexual issues, knowledge of the sexual trends in our teens' world helps us to share the truth about sex in light of God's plan. Though they are aware of sex in a way that we might not have been at their age, our goal is not to teach about sex but about how they can make choices based on their worth to God. For this to occur, parents must be able to communicate by showing that they are available and accepting and love their teens enough to provide a safe environment for ongoing conversation. It won't happen with lectures about what not to do, because these teens are familiar with the girl who walks down the hallway with a diaper bag in one hand and a backpack in the other. They understand the term "my baby's daddy." They need to hear the balancing messages about sex and God's plan for a lifetime of intimacy.

I think it is true that sex before marriage is not portrayed as bad, but that doesn't mean that we have to give in to it. True, a lot have, but a lot haven't! It does affect me in the way that it seems almost weird and out of the norm to say you're going to stay true to your future spouse, but no matter what's going on around me, I want to save myself for marriage.

Janelle T., age 16

Sex is only one of many issues that have changed since you were a teen. Let's look at other matters that affect this generation and the way that they perceive God and faith.

SPIRITUALITY VERSUS CHRISTIANITY

Question: Do you think that those who are not believers see Christianity in a negative light?

I think the world sees Christians as helpless people who are weak enough to need to believe in something and as naïve people who don't realize the truth shown in science and other disciplines. Unless God prepares their hearts, people view things this way.

Sarah C., age 19

It is easy to find yourself living in a sheltered world where you believe that everyone attends church. Yet one trip to the local discount store on a Sunday morning will dispel that belief. There is a vast majority of good people who live, love, raise families, work, and exist without the influence of the church. An increasing number of people have very little contact with, or understanding of, the Christian faith. A large percentage of adults have never attended a Christian church. Others have left in search of spirituality that does not include Christianity. They disagree with a faith that embraces absolutes and the teaching that Christ is the only way to salvation. Many of these adults are now bringing up a second generation that does not know God as a personal Savior or is unsure of what that means.

Relativism is something that has crept into our society and into our teens' lives. There are many definitions of a postmodern culture, but a simple definition is "a society without absolutes." Relativism says that truth is conditional. It says that there are many ways to God, and Christianity is only one of many choices. Therefore, we live in a spiritual nation, but not necessarily a Christian nation.

The picture of Christianity for unbelievers is confusing. Is Christianity what you view on religious programming, or is it what you see in your neighbor who attends church every Sunday? The lines are blurred for unbelievers as nominal Christians talk about God and yet live no differently than those who do not profess faith. Barna Research Group said:

> We find a growing willingness among Americans to embrace all theology as equally valid, regardless of the genesis of the theology. The consequence is a watering down of Christian theology to such a low standard that it often conflicts with, rather than conforms to, Scripture.[6]

The Barna study reports that only three out of ten self-described Christian teenagers claim to be "absolutely committed" to the Christian faith.[7] Because of this, Christianity is no longer perceived in a positive light in America. An unbelieving world does not understand a faith that can be shared on a T-shirt or WWJD bracelet but not be etched on a committed lifestyle.

Some days we feel like we just don't fit in. God is the only one who cares or understands; he knows what it is like. No one seems to understand. The world is so messed up, and we, as Christians, don't seem to fit in.

Brianna B., age 16

What about committed Christian teens? They must overcome these hurdles as well as live their faith in an environment that does not nurture or support their beliefs. They cannot wear masks. They are challenged, provoked, and questioned about their faith. Sometimes they encounter hostility and are perceived as intolerant or as "haters."

WHO IS MY FAMILY?

Every teen struggles with something; for me it's my broken family.

Brianna B., age 16

The family structure has changed significantly since you were a teen. Single or divorced moms or dads, single parents with live-in partners, guardians, grandparents, gay or lesbian couples, foster homes, and adoptive families raise millions of children. Family relationships have changed so much that the Supreme Court was asked in January of 2000 to redefine the legal boundaries of what "family" means.[8] Though family relationships have changed, the importance of family in our teens' lives has not.

In America we have almost ditched the term "family," but family is important. It is the root of who you are. If your family is broken, you are broken inside—unless you find God's family. If your family is whole, you can be more secure in who you are and in your future. Family does not have to be a mom and a dad. Family is built on love.

Anna A., age 15

If our teens don't find what they need in the family unit, they look for it elsewhere. This generation is open to the message of love. They embrace the concept of a heavenly Father who will never leave you or forsake you. Unfortunately, many young women are also open to a message of love from any male, leaving them vulnerable to accept a form of love that does not satisfy their needs. Many young men find acceptance in groups that define love as loyalty, brotherhood, and strength in numbers. They offer their allegiance at all cost, simply to have a place where they are received and acknowledged.

Parents need to remember that they have a huge influence on kids. If kids see their parents fighting, they'll think that's how marriage is. If the parents take the easy way out by saying they aren't in love anymore, then kids may think, "They will leave me when they've known me too long." Or the kids will learn that things don't work out perfectly and just give up. Divorce can be necessary in some situations, but a marriage is supposed to be forever, and divorce does have huge consequences for the kids and family. My parents are divorced, and it was really difficult for a while because they wouldn't even talk to each other. Then I stopped seeing my dad, which was hard for a while. I'm okay with it now. After several years I have my own life and I don't miss my dad much, although I miss feeling like a whole family.

Sarah C., age 19

Divorce is at an all-time high in the United States. More than one million children have parents who separate or divorce each year.[9] Teens and children must adjust as their family units change to embrace stepparents, new siblings, and/or stepsiblings or as they move away from familiar surroundings.

A family is a group of people who you love—people you'd do anything for. They don't have to be blood. They can be close friends. Sometimes friends are closer family than blood kin.

Mary R., age 17

The Supreme Court is not the only group that has redefined family. Only a handful of teens described family as a mom and dad and siblings. Many characterized family as feelings—security, love, and acceptance. Some described family as doing things together or people who are related and love to laugh and be with each other. Most teens defined family as any person who offers consistent love, acceptance, and stability.

I guess you could define family as your relatives, but most of all … unconditional love.

Michelle A., age 19

These definitions offer a distinctly different perspective than the traditional viewpoint of family. For every teen, family—no matter what the definition—is important. Because the family is so vital to the stability and well-being of teens, we'll dive deeper into that subject in a later chapter.

Technology—The Good, Bad, and Ugly

I feel apart from the world. I think it may have to do with the generation that we live in and the fact that we just sit in front of the computer and TV.

Grace B., age 13

Today's teens are surrounded by gadgets including cell phones, IM (Instant Messaging), chat rooms, MP3 players, computer and video games, web cams, the Internet, text messaging, and e-mail, just to name a few. Teens can scour the Internet for scholarships and find research on any subject. They are very aware of, and comfortable with, other countries and cultures. They are facilitators of tons of useful and useless information. Teens can check their e-mail, play computer games with people in their neighborhoods or in other nations, chat with friends through instant messaging, and download their favorite songs all at the same time. They are the ultimate multi-taskers.

These technological advances have also produced teens (and adults) who interact more easily with people in a chat room than with a family member in the next room. Technological advances have made pornography accessible with the click of a mouse.

They are right when they say we are a disconnected generation. I know I'm disconnected, and sometimes it's just easier to stay that way.

Mercy D., age 15

There is one aspect of technology that these advances have achieved that is rarely discussed, which is that today's teens don't truly know how to be alone. They are surrounded by a plethora of technological toys, and many of them don't know how to unplug. Silence is not golden to today's teens; it's unsettling. Unsettling silence is why many teens lull themselves to sleep with the television. It's why you see teens with headphones on in the midst of a crowd.

The technology at our fingertips allows us to talk to youth across the globe, but we are unable to open our hearts to the youth next door.

Helen V., age 16

This phenomenon affects many teens' prayer lives because it's hard to find a place where they can be alone with God. My daughter, Melissa, called a friend to see if he wanted to hang out later. "What are you doing?" she asked.

"I was praying," he replied.

"Then why did you answer the phone?"

Good question. This young man was searching for a

deeper prayer life. He felt distracted. Finding alone time with God seemed impossible. Turning the phone off never occurred to him until that moment.

Many teens feel overwhelmed and stressed. We challenged the youth in our church to unplug and find a secret place with God. This had nothing to do with location, but with pushing out all the hype and noise so that they could communicate with a living God. Several teens reported that they felt anxious as they sat in a quiet room. They wanted to do something to fill the dead air. Anything but silence. Yet they took the challenge because they wanted to feel God and to hear from him. Each teen took his relationship to a deeper level. It took time, but they found that they could not only be comfortable alone, but that there was rest and peace once they were unplugged.

Violence

Question: Do you believe that you face more violence than previous generations?

The parents think it's [violence] a problem because people are always saying that what us teens watch on TV is going to "make us" do as we see. We are used to it and don't care. We know that we are our own person (at least most of us do).

Adam D., age 18

Has violence changed since you were a teen? This was the most polarized subject of any discussed. The polls, statistics, and adult viewpoints said one thing. Teens said something completely different. Whether teens feel safe or not has little to do with the things that bother adults the most: violence in media, graphic video games, violent lyrics, school shootings, road rage, and increased statistics of violence in the home and at school. If violence personally affected a teen, then he reported his world as violent. If not, then he felt safe.

I've been bullied at school to the point that my life has been verbally and physically threatened. We have had a school shooting.

Mary R., age 18

The vast majority of schools are safe. Yet for those who experienced the horrific nightmare of school shootings, their perception of safety was forever altered. Several students in our youth group attend a school in Ft. Gibson, Oklahoma. When they were in middle school a classmate brought a gun to school and wounded several classmates, some critically. Though no one was killed, the students' image of physical well-being was never the same after that moment.

However, schools are safe for most teens. Incidences such as Columbine have prompted schools and communities to take measures to ensure student safety. The overall rate of school violence has fallen.[10] Fewer students are carrying weapons to school, and school shootings account for less than two percent of student violence. Students are more apt to encounter bullying, physical fights, and threatening or hostile remarks than full-blown violence.

Question: What about the graphic violence on television? It bothers me as an adult, but it seems that teens barely notice it—even when it's really gruesome. Why do you think that parents think it's a problem, but teens don't?

We've seen violence our whole lives. It's just something you get used to watching. Our parents never had that much growing up, so they don't understand.

April W., age 14

What I discovered was that the perception of violence has definitely changed since the dark ages when we were teenagers. What I consider violent and horrific, today's teens barely give a second glance.

Parents care for their children and don't want them to see stuff like that. But teens don't really care that much for themselves, so they watch it anyway. They think that it won't happen to them, that the movies won't really have an affect on them.

Mandy H., age 17

I had a conversation with several Christian teens about this subject. They laughed at my innocence. I tried to explain how I was concerned about violence as a mom and as someone who loves teens. "Suzie, it's not that bad. You guys are all worked up over television, and that's not even the real problem facing teens."

Depression and Suicide

The biggest problem for me is depression and hurting myself. My parents could not stop me from hurting myself. I would never tell them why I do it. I think the truth is that as teenagers we don't even know. We use hurting ourselves as a way to deal with stress, pain, and annoyance.

Grace B., age 13

This is an area of violence to which teens do relate. During the process of writing this book, two young women—former classmates of my oldest daughter—died as a result of suicide. Both deaths stunned me. I could see their faces in my mind. It was hard to grasp the fact that they had come to a point in their lives when death seemed like a good alternative.

Youth suicide is a major public health problem in the United States.[11] The overall suicide rate has declined over the past twenty years, but the suicide rate for teens fifteen to nineteen years old has increased by six percent. For adolescents ten to fourteen years old, the suicide rate increased by more than one hundred percent over the past twenty years.[12] Suicide is the third leading cause of death for young people ages ten to nineteen.

Parents and the church need to teach young people that you can't base things on emotion, because in the end they will leave you feeling empty and lonely. For me, when I get that awful feeling, the number-one thing I want is for someone to hug me and let me know that they care.

Beth R., age 17

Question: The statistics say that your generation faces overwhelming loneliness. Do you believe that?

Some of us have been hurt. We hold everything in. We constantly hide our true selves. When someone tries to get close to us, we move away. We think that will stop us from getting hurt, when in the long run it kills us emotionally.

Pete D., age 18

"What in the world do teens have to be depressed about? They have everything!" one parent commented recently.

"All I want is for my teen to be happy," said another parent. "I've given her things that I never had as a teen, and she's still not happy."

There are a lot of teens out there that feel that way. Parents are working to get more money to afford their houses, or college, and to buy their kids things; but maybe they should work less and spend more time with their teens. The teens will remember the time that the parents spent with them, not the things they bought for them.

Michelle H., age 18

Giving our teens things is not a cure for the loneliness, depression, and emptiness that plague this generation. The need is simple: love. It's not about self-esteem, success, or achievements. It's not about gifts or new cars. It's about unselfish, sacrificial love that can never be gift-wrapped.

I think it's because of the way families are these days, so many divorced parents and children being raised by only one parent. I think this makes them lean toward drugs, scandal, and many other things, and this makes them even lonelier. All of the things they look to only make them lonely when they really should be looking to the one that could cure that empty spot in their hearts: God. And I also feel that Christians are not reaching out enough in this generation. We need to reach out and set better examples for the ones who refuse him time and time again.

Jen W., age 15

This generation, more than any other, has been given so many definitions of love, and yet the deeper meaning of love has been diminished. They have lost something of great value and are not sure what it is. Yet they are looking for it.

Most teens described loneliness or depression as emptiness, a void in their lives.

I often experience this type of loneliness. I can be surrounded by family and know that God and my friends are there yet feel so alone and desperate for someone to love me. It's like having a huge void that nothing can fill.

Becky S., age 18

The October 2002 issue of *Newsweek* reported that 3 million adolescents were depressed, citing causes including rising divorce rates and social pressure. Ten years ago depression was considered an adult disease, but today it is viewed as chronic in teens. Some health professionals have termed it as epidemic. When I shared these statistics with a group of teens, every single teen said the numbers were wrong. I was encouraged—until I realized they meant that the numbers were too low. "It's got to be more like one in five," said one teen.

If you are not accepted for who you are, you are lost—even to yourself.

Anna A., age 15

STOP!

If after reading this chapter, you decide to grab your teen and build an underground shelter to escape society, then I've failed. Not every teen is confronted with cyber stalkers, school violence, dysfunctional families, or sexual meltdowns. Not every teen is lonely or depressed. We discussed these issues in this chapter because if parents want to connect with their teens, they need to be educated. Sometimes adults are tempted to discredit that which they fear or feel ignorant about.

This *is* your teen's youth culture. Though every aspect of modern teenage life will not apply to your teen, these issues do impact him or her. When your teen shuts his eyes and clenches his teeth and says, "You just don't understand!" he's not trying to push you away. Chances are you *don't* understand. You can pierce your eyebrow, shave your head, or get a cool tattoo, but that doesn't draw you closer to the world of your teen. The information in this chapter can refocus you as a parent. It can help you to spotlight the important things.

Have things changed since you were a teen? Yes! Should you react in fear? No! There were things that scared your parents, and see how far you've come? Your mom or dad might have railed against your music, and yet you continue to hum along with it in elevators to this day.

Think back for a moment. What would have happened if your parents had tried to see your world from a different point of view than their own? What would have happened if they had understood what you were really facing and reached out to you on that level?

Intriguing thought, isn't it?

MAKE IT REAL

Partner in Prayer

Pray for your child every day. Ask God to protect his or her heart, mind, and body. Cover your teen with prayer for strength and the ability to make beneficial choices.

Pray for those who come in contact with your teen. Ask God to bless your teen's youth pastor and his ministry. Pray for your teen's teachers. Pray for his or her friends.

If your teen is struggling, ask God to give you wisdom to see beyond the surface issues. Ask God to help you see your teen as he sees your teen—as a seeker and as a potential child of God. Ask him to give you strength and knowledge and faith to believe in what you cannot see—yet.

RESOURCES

Study resources that speak directly to your teen about issues that matter to him. The following are just a few of the many books and magazines available that discuss real-world youth issues.

Real Teens, Real Stories, Real Life by T. Suzanne Eller (RiverOak Publishing)–Real-life stories from teens who experienced pain and triumph. From pornography to homosexuality to body image, teens share their experiences and how they met a God who changed their lives forever.

The Youth Builder: Reach Young People for Christ and Change Lives Forever by Jim Burns, Ph.D., with Mike DeVries (Gospel Light Publications)—Written for youth workers, and with invaluable information about relational issues, contemporary topics, and practical insights.

Real Teens: A Contemporary Snapshot of Youth Culture by George Barna (Regal Books)—Barna Research Group interviewed teens on issues such as faith and spirituality, family, race, and other current topics that affect teenagers.

Passageway.org (http://passageway.org)—Billy Graham online youth magazine with articles, devotions, and contemporary teen topics.

Relevant Magazine (http://www.relevantmagazine.com)—Christian youth magazine discussing progressive culture including music, media, books, and faith.

Barna Research Online (http://www.barna.org)—Christian research organization with articles, statistics, and information on contemporary issues that affect faith and Christians.

Chapter Three

Your Teen's Cluster

Why love if losing hurts so much?
We love to know that we are not alone.
—C. S. Lewis

Question: If you had a choice of being popular or having three to five good friends, which would you choose?

Three to five friends! It's better to be loved for who you are than for who you are not.

Mandy H., age 18

A cluster is defined as a group of three to five people who will accept you for who you are. They are people you can count on and with whom your presence is always welcome.

Today's teens desire to surround themselves with people they can depend upon. Having a cluster is more important than gaining the approval of the majority of their peers. This goes against the image of the stereotypical teen vying for a spot at the popular lunch table. Not only do they not worry about whether the popular crowd is going to let them sit with them; many teens avoid that table altogether.

I have three to five fantastic friends who mean the world to me. I find this to be a better situation because you grow closer. There is always someone there to support you. It's closer-knit. Being popular has never appealed to me, because you have to conform to other people's ideas and values and not your own. You become popular for thinking the same way as the popular crowd.

Louise C., age 16

The cluster has taken a prominent place in teens' lives because they gravitate to those who accept them. If teens do not feel welcome in their churches, their youth groups, or families, they will leave—physically or emotionally—and find a cluster that will accept them. Relationships are crucial to this generation, though they struggle with them. This is why they look for loyal relationships rather than settle for popularity.

I would choose three to five friends because they love you and are loyal to you no matter what.

Hannah M., age 16

Overall, today's youth have a hard time building relationships because they struggle with the cultural definition of issues such as commitment, conflict resolution, and intimacy. Popular culture sends a message that people live by feelings. If you feel attracted to another person, then it's natural to go with that feeling even if you are with someone else. If someone hurts you, then burn that relationship and move on to the next. Intimacy is defined as attraction or sexual compatibility, leaving out the ingredients of friendship, marriage vows, love, and constancy.

Today's teens are not the first generation to accept this philosophy of living by feelings. Their parents' generation embraced it; therefore, many teens have been hurt and are skeptical.

I saw a lot of things in my life that I wish I had never seen. It's behind me now, but I will never allow my kids to see such things in me.

Annie T., age 18

You must earn your way into your teen's heart, and if you betray his trust, he will quickly shut you out. I'm often asked how I persuade teens to accept me as an adult. It has nothing to do with them accepting me. The way to break the shell of skepticism around the heart of a teen is simple: unconditional love. If teens know that someone believes in them and genuinely sees them as people of worth, they will respond. I encounter all types of teens. Some are hurt and hardened. Many are friendly and inviting. Some teens are immature, while others are wise beyond their years. Yet there is one constant among all of them: Teens want to be loved for who they are.

I'm not blind to teens' faults, and they are not blind to mine. I'm transparent with them. They know that there are times when I'm an absolute dork. They know that I love God and that I'm a seeker, but I will never attain perfection. They know that I'm in my forties and I'm neither hip nor cool. None of these things matters to these teens, because they know that I love them for who they are.

I am honest with them. If I see a teen making a mistake that will harm her or others, I'm not afraid to encourage her to make a better choice. She receives that advice from me because she knows that I will fight for her and believe in her. She understands that I see something of value in her—even when she messes up.

We are the group that no one sees except when we do something wrong.

Ben N., age 14

Teens will not hand their hearts to the first adult that says the words "I love you." They often feel disrespected because they are pushed to accept being labeled in a way that doesn't clearly define who they are. They are skeptics. They hear so many words, but actions let them know if you are real—and that takes time.

My mom loves me, but I haven't seen my dad in years. I'm not sure if he loves me. I'm not sure if he realizes that love is an action.

Sarah C., age 19

A group of teens attend our youth services every Wednesday night. They are not typical churched teens. These teens smoke in the parking lot, confront authority, and keep us all on our knees in prayer. They live in a rough part of our city. Our biggest problem is not sharing the gospel with them. Our biggest problem is keeping them in the youth theater until the service is over.

Our goal is to take every teen in the youth group to the next level in their relationships with God. With these troubled teens, we are not shooting for discipleship at this point. Our goal is to make them feel comfortable enough that they will stay for an entire service. That's the next level for them spiritually. It's not even about salvation yet, because they aren't receptive. We are still in the process of earning their trust, and we won't impact their souls until we reach them on a personal level. To believe, they have to feel as if they belong.

You see, they don't understand. They hear church people talk about the love of God, but then these teens go home to very different situations. Many question why God exists at church or in other teens' families but fails to show up at their houses. One young man lives with his mom and her female lover. Another teen lives next door to a crack house. She has a single mom that must work two jobs. This mother is doing the best she can by herself because the girl's father is nowhere in the picture.

These teens are angry, and they don't care what I, or anybody else, thinks. They've been taught to live by feelings, and they will quickly sell out tomorrow for today. I've had to take crowbars out of teens' hands in a parking lot to stop a fight. I've climbed into empty church vans and broken up teens that were definitely not seeking God. I've sat down beside a group of teens and felt like the unpopular kid in middle school when they all stood up in unison and left. It's hard to put your arm around a teen and have her push you away.

It would be easy to give up, but we can't because these teens need a cluster, and we'd like to be that cluster. One day they will be ready for answers, and we want them to feel that they can come to us. Then we will have the opportunity to lead them to Christ. Then we can disciple them. But they will only allow us to help them spiritually as far as they trust our motives. If they think we love their souls, but not them, we don't have a chance.

Keeping this in mind is paying off. The same girl who pushed me away now voluntarily gives me a hug every week. If I sit down with these teens in youth service, they don't move away anymore. Some are glad that I want to hang out with them. Some of them now like me a lot, but they only let me know that when their friends aren't around.

I believe loneliness is huge in my generation because we are a very emotional culture. Everything is based on feelings and what feels good at the moment.

Beth R., age 17

Let's be honest. It's hard to continue to reach out to someone when your efforts are rebuffed. Our instinct is to react in anger or hostility when a teen puts up a shield and pushes us away. When adults react in anger, they enter a playing field for which they are unequipped and at which the teen is a master. The fight is over before it even begins.

If my parents could do one thing to impact my faith it would be to act like Jesus would—even if it feels weird.

Jessica L., age 14

Do you want to disarm teens? Love them unconditionally. It's scriptural. Unconditional love is given to us every single day. We receive selfless mercy and love from God even when we don't deserve it. Giving that same love to teens who don't expect it shows them Christ in a way that words cannot. It breaks down the barriers one brick at a time.

You first have to accept us before we'll be open to any of your advice, no matter how good it might be.

Janelle T., age 15

It's hard work to penetrate teens' hearts when they've learned at a young age about selfishness, abuse, and betrayal. It's not much easier with the teens who seem to have it all. They live in the same world as the troubled teens and are conditioned with similar messages. Real relationships take time, patience, and a willingness to love your teen even when he is unlovable. The question for every parent becomes: Are you in your child's cluster?

Loving someone—no matter what. That is my definition of family.

Melissa A., age 18

The Family Cluster

Question: How would you define family?

A place where a child can feel safe and loved.

Heather Y., age 18

When asked to define family, teens overwhelmingly defined family as love. The family cluster is an environment where each member has the opportunity to be nurtured. It is where members can turn when they need guidance or comfort. It's where each person can strive for excellence without having to be perfect. It is your teen's refuge.

A family is a loving environment, whether it is real parents or aunts or another family.

Michelle H., age 17

Unfortunately families do not always function in this manner. We live in a society where the strength of families is fractured.

My home is not a safe place. I am always worried that my parents will be in a bad mood and that I will get yelled at. My parents usually fight, and my dad and I have our differences. I know they love me. They just have a hard time showing it.

Elizabeth B., age 17

Fractured families are one of the reasons that youth are wide open to receiving the message of the gospel. Initially, they are intrigued by the story of a man rejected by the mainstream, but it is the message of unconditional love that draws them in.

Tell parents that it is worth it to love their kids unconditionally, because it's something we don't get often. It is the one thing that will greatly impact our lives.

Stan T., age 15

What does it mean to be in your child's cluster? Does it mean that you drop the role of parent and become your teen's best friend? Your teen has friends, but he needs you as a parent. Parents offer boundaries and structure. Parents provide discipline, encouragement, and guidance. How do you do that and still become a part of your teen's cluster?

If parents want to help kids to not feel lonely, they can love us and prove to us that we're loved and accepted for who we are. They can let us know that we don't have to change to get our parents' love. That's what I need anyway.

Janelle T., age 16

Building friendships with your teen might seem like a balancing act. Sometimes, being a parent means that you love your teen enough to let him be angry with you—if making an unpopular decision is in his best interest. But the concrete in your long-lasting relationship from your kid's teen years to adulthood will be consistent love. It will be an affirmation of his value to you.

If parents have a great friendship with their teens, they [the teens] will not want to go behind the parents' backs or rebel. Discipline without friendship never works. That's what makes teens bitter. We don't want to feel judged, condemned, or accused. We want to feel accepted and have a friendship with our parents. We want to feel comfortable talking with our parents about anything, to be able to laugh and have a good time with them. Quality time. Love.

Michelle H., age 17

Every parent's goal is to eventually be friends with her teen. My children are in college, and I love the fact that we are at a different level in our relationships now. At first I wasn't sure how to deal with it. My oldest daughter, Leslie, came home to visit during her freshman year. It was a Friday night, and we assumed that she would be going out with friends. Richard and I went out to eat, and when we came back she said, "I wish you guys would have invited me. I would have loved to have gone."

"I never dreamed that you would want to hang out with us on a Friday night," I replied. We laughed, realizing that something had changed in our relationship. Though we had always loved each other's company, Friday nights were definitely not reserved for Mom or Dad. Today when my teens come home, their friends pile in at our house, but my children also look forward to the moments that we have as a family.

DARE TO BELIEVE

I'm not the horrible kid that they think I am. Sometimes I think that they think that only because I am somewhat disorganized. They seem to think that makes me a bad kid, and I'm really not.

Ashley B., age 14

Do you remember being dared in elementary school? Someone challenged you to do something that seemed impossible, and you stepped up to the plate to prove that you were capable. Teens are hoping that their parents will dare to believe in them.

My mom has totally impacted my life with her optimism for my life. If I told her that I was going to the moon, she would believe me and be behind me all the way.

Michelle H., age 17

Finding your way into your teen's cluster happens when you look beyond the obvious. Teens are looking for someone to see their potential. Don't confuse this with the insincere self-esteem theology that is as transparent as it is faulty, or the pressurized push to achieve success. Teens simply want Mom and Dad to see their hearts and to believe with them that they are people of value.

My parents trust me. I have not always been trustworthy, but I think my parents know that it has always been in my heart to honor them.

Keith J., age 21

At times, parenting is frustrating and discouraging. I've had moments when I confessed to God that I had no clue. Yet God is faithful. He helps us when we are unsure. He helps us to dare to believe that our children will become what God intended from the very beginning.

Do you dare to believe?

Make It Real

Word Games

1. If you were to describe your family, what words would you use? Is your family close? Are you fun loving? Are your relationships built on genuine love and respect? Would you describe your family as alienated? Angry? Embattled? Autonomous?

   It's time to be honest. Write down five words that describe your family.

   ____________________ ____________________

   ____________________ ____________________

   ____

2. Write down something positive about each member of your family. Be genuine. Ask God to help you look beyond the surface.

____________________ ____________________

____________________ ____________________

____________________ ____________________

____________________ ____________________

3. Using what you've written above, pray in specific terms. Praise God for the positive traits in your family and in each family member. Ask for God's help in the exact areas that need his intervention.

Chapter Four

How's Your Day?

Words are, of course, the most powerful drug used by mankind.
—Rudyard Kipling

Question: How much time do you talk to your mom or dad each day?
Does it go ever go deeper than, "How's your day?"

You should be able to honestly talk to your parents.
Mika W., age 17

"How's your day?" These are the first words heard in most homes when someone walks through the door. But what happens next?

I have never met a parent who doesn't long to talk to his teen. One frustrated dad cornered me at a conference. "How can I know what my teen is facing if she won't talk to me?" he asked. That conversation reminded me of a cartoon I'd seen once. A mother stood behind her teenaged son. She ran a can opener over his head and glanced inside. When he turned to her with an annoyed expression, she threw up her hands and said, "I just wanted to see what you're thinking!"

Can you relate? Talking with your teen can be a roller coaster experience with both highs and lows as you try to connect with your child. The irony is that teens all over the nation are saying that they are not content with chitchat or "Turn down that music!"

My mom and I often do mission work together, and while we are working we talk about every subject you can think of.

Esther M., age 17

It's rewarding when you can be open with your teen and talk about deeper issues. Yet many parent-teen relationships have a definite gap in the channel of communication. It's especially painful when a parent knows that her child is open with others. The bottom line is that it's important to develop good communication skills, because a teen just might have something important to say.

If I could tell my mother and father something and they promised not to interrupt or pass judgment or yell, I would tell them all the times I've lied to them, the times I said I was going places that I never went, how I told them all about movies I'd never seen. I would tell them about my last relationship, the stuff that they don't know. I would tell them about the time when we left the school dance and went to a secluded part in the woods and how he tried to make me do things I didn't want to do. I'd tell them how hard it was when he was telling me what he wanted to do and how I said no and how he pressured me more than I could take. I'd tell them how I cried myself to sleep every night and how he told me I was nothing and didn't deserve anything, how he told me that I was a hypocrite whenever I wouldn't do any sexual things, how I came so close to losing my virginity. I'd tell my mom that her stupid curfew kept me safe. I'd tell them how he left bruises on my arms and how when I asked him if he loved me, he would say, "I guess so, as much as anyone really can." I would tell them I was sorry for breaking the rules, for bending them and wanting them changed. I would tell them that even though I thought the rules were stupid then, they kept me safe. I'd tell my parents that, because of them, I'm okay now.

Amber L., age 17

Would Somebody Please Help Me?

A parent approached me and handed me a note. "It's my daughter's phone number," she said. "I want you to call her. She won't come to church. She's hanging out with some older guy. I've tried to tell her that I'm worried about her, but anytime I try to talk to her she just stands there. I figured that if she wouldn't talk to me, she might talk to you. I give up!"

I had observed their dialogue before. It resembled a chess match. Each move was designed to pin the other person into a corner. It was a test to see who could come back with the quickest jab or the most hurtful putdown. This mother and daughter had learned unhealthy patterns of conversation that did not allow them to develop trust and intimacy, yet both of them longed to be close. The mother saw her daughter's silence as rejection and became angry. The daughter saw her mother's attempts at talking as prying, so she withdrew. It was a frustrating cycle.

We never go deeper than "How's your day?" unless I have some explaining to do.

Diana C., age 16

Parents were not given a "How to Talk to Your Teen" handbook when their infants were placed in their arms. They are thrust into a different world when their children approach their teen years. Suddenly, they are no longer their children's ultimate influence. Their teens develop close friendships with others and expand their world to include activities, events, and people that are outside the family unit. A parent vies with the world to gain the confidence of his teen. This is the time when your conversational skills will be tested.

My dad is really tough. He loves to be in control, and when he gets mad, he'll yell. That's exactly how he was raised, and although he's working on it, sometimes it still shows through.

Katie H., age 15

Many of the mistakes that parents make are a result of how they interacted with their own parents. If our parents represented total authority in our lives and conversation was considered backtalk or disrespectful, we might introduce that same pattern into our own relationships with our teens. The opposite can also happen when a parent who was unable to talk with her own parents now uses her teen as her best friend and tells her everything—even burdens that the teen might not be equipped to bear. If conversation was nonexistent between you and your parents, then it might be a struggle to know where to begin between you and your teen. We offer our children all that we know, but sometimes it doesn't seem like enough. It's disappointing when you attempt to initiate conversation and are rejected. It's even more frustrating when you are unsure of the reason for the rejection.

Ignorance is not bliss. That's a tired cliché. Knowing and understanding the mistakes that cause communication to shut down gives us the opportunity for change. Knowing and understanding helps us to explore different methods to communicate with our teens and destroy barriers that have hindered real conversation in the past. These barriers are things that we parents do that push away our teens. Most of the time parents are unaware that they've even done something offensive. Parents' conversational skills can invite their children in or can stop conversations cold. We discussed keys to effective listening in a previous chapter, but let's look at six mistakes that might keep us from communicating effectively with our teens.

Mistake #1—Not Sticking to the Issue

Question: How do the things that your parents say affect you?

When they express their faith in me to do the right thing and succeed, it makes it easier to succeed. When they tell me what I do right and praise my good qualities and talents, it helps to strengthen them.

Keith J., age 21

One time when we were with a group of adult friends our conversation centered on our teens. A father shared a story of a conflict he had had with his daughter the night before. She was going out with friends and had entered the room wearing a shirt that left too little to the imagination. Her father ordered her to change the shirt, and as she left the room, he commented, "You look like a whore when you dress like that."

If it's bad, it makes me feel bad. If it's good, then it makes me feel special or something.

Patience D., age 17

Several of our friends looked up in surprise, and the father defended his comment by saying, "They were only words. My daughter knows I didn't mean it. Besides, she had no business wearing that shirt."

Good things lift my spirits and make me really happy, but bad things—they make me feel like trash.

Serina-Linn C., age 16

Words can start wars. Words can tear down and rip apart, build up or shape individuals. Words have the power to spur us to greatness. Words are one thing that we can give freely, but we can never take back once they are spoken.

A lot of times my dad has said really derogatory comments to my brothers, and every single one of those incidents is engraved in my brain. I can't forget it, even if I wanted to. Some of the things that my dad has said to me put me down just or make me feel stupid.

Mercy D., age 15

Contrary to this father's opinion, his words were costly.

He is the man that his daughter looks to for guidance and love. Her self-esteem is built on his actions and upon his words. She will see herself in the eyes of other men according to her father's love, or lack thereof. The words he spoke didn't fit the situation or his daughter. The matter of the shirt became secondary as he assaulted her character. He later apologized and shared with his daughter the reasons why he didn't want her to wear the shirt. They were sound, and she accepted them, but the sting of his words was already etched upon her soul. We are accountable for the words that we speak.

Separating the actions from the person is difficult at times, but it's crucial. Our words are our primary method of communication with our loved ones. Humiliation is not an effective tool for discipline, but it is a powerful way to damage your relationships. Words leave a legacy—and legacies aren't always positive. Legacies can be damaging and carried from generation to generation. If your parents spoke to you in a manner that was harmful, stop the cycle. You can use the past as an excuse, or you can realize that you are making your children's memories now.

Everything a parent says affects his children. It usually determines a child's self-confidence.

Melissa E., age 19

What do you hope to achieve? Do you want your words to motivate? Do you want your teen to see the situation from a different perspective? Do you want to correct his behaviors? Do you hope to prompt your teen to positive action? What is the real problem, and what are the specific actions you want from your teen? Tossing out words like shrapnel can hurt your teen. Sticking to the issue allows you to offer specific and clear instructions to guide her.

Mistake #2—Labeling

Whenever I would make my mom upset or angry, she would say that I was mean, cold, and hateful. Eventually I started believing her, and I started to hate myself. It's hard to want to live when you hate yourself.

Lara M., age 16

There is a theory called the Looking Glass Self. It states that people see themselves in light of how others see them. It doesn't matter what the real mirror says. When a person consistently hears negative reactions, those labels become his reality. To demonstrate this I asked several teens in my discipleship class to form a circle. Two students, Rudy and Tara, stood in the circle, facing each other. I instructed Rudy to pretend that something was wrong with Tara's face. The class was aware of this, but Tara was not. As the interview progressed, Rudy fidgeted and glanced at Tara, but quickly looked away. Tara wiped at her nose. She looked down at the floor. Eventually she burst out in frustration. "What is wrong with you? Is there something wrong with my face?" She was relieved (and forgave me) when I explained the Looking Glass Self theory and explained that she and Rudy had demonstrated the theory perfectly. She had made an assumption about herself based on Rudy's reactions.

If their words are encouraging, I am always happy. But if

something negative is said, it makes me feel like I'm the lowest thing on earth (thankfully this rarely happens).

Salena B., age 18

Youth are labeled in many ways. *Preppie, techie, freak, goth, hot, skank, jock,* and *snob* are only a few of the labels. These labels will change tomorrow, but the effects do not. Labels push people into predefined roles that might have little to do with the individuals in reality.

There are many ways that teens are labeled. They are labeled by what they wear and what they look like. I can tell you every skinny joke known to man. In high school I was 5' 6" and weighed less than 100 pounds. I was called "Stretch," "Olive Oyl," and "Bones," just to name a few. Once I was on the school bus and we passed a gas station. It had a large sign in front that said, "We fix flats." A thirteen-year-old classmate pointed in my direction and said, "Suzie, you ought to stop in." The group that sat at the back of the bus erupted in rowdy laughter while I clutched my backpack to my chest. I was humiliated, but I didn't let them know how much it hurt, because that would have only opened the door for additional embarrassment. I simply let it go.

Teens are labeled by their backgrounds. What do their parents do for a living? What kind of car can they afford to drive? What kind of house do they have? What kind of family do they come from? With all of these characterizations, the last place they need to find additional labels is in their own homes. Reinforcement—whether positive or negative—shapes the way our teens see themselves. Teens will attempt to live up to our views of them—whether they are good or bad.

The only thing that ever hurts me is something my mother says. I am very independent, and she reminds me that I am incapable of keeping any relationships because of my independence. She has told me since I was thirteen that I am incapable of allowing anyone to show affection or of allowing someone to care for me. This stems from the fact that I stopped sharing my life with my mother at thirteen because all I received in return was destructive criticism. She thought that the blockade of emotions that I built between us to protect myself from getting hurt was a trait that I had in all my relationships. This constant verbal battering actually ran into my relationships. I became insecure with my friends and the opposite sex. It is a battle that at twenty years old I am finally beginning to conquer with God's help.

Lacynda B., age 20

What the crowd thinks is of little importance. Your teen's background, whether privileged or not, doesn't make him higher or lower in God's eyes. Looks fade away. We have the opportunity to teach our teens that they are significant simply because God knows them by name. Our words are powerful, for we shape our children when they look into our reflections and see that they are of worth to God—because they are of worth to us.

My mom told me that I am everything that she wished she was when she was my age. I think about that on a week-to-week basis.

Becca A., age 15

Mistake #3—Failing to Encourage

My parents are generally positive people, so most everything they say encourages me.

Esther M., age 17

Years ago I had a boss who would throw papers on secretaries' desks if he found a typo. I took pride in my work, and when he did this to me, it made me feel small. He only noticed the one percent of mistakes that were made and never commented on the ninety-nine percent of positive contributions from the office staff. His responses made me want to quit. Every person deserves to be treated with dignity, even when he makes a mistake.

When I am a parent, I will be different. I know what things my parents have done as they brought me up and how it has made me rebellious. I would be a bit less harsh on a lot of levels and encourage them [my kids] in everything.

Steven S., age 16

We know that words affect our teens, but what about the words we fail to speak?

Do our teens realize that they are loved, even when they are struggling? Do we affirm them? We are often quick to talk about what they do wrong, but do we let them know what they do right?

My mom was complaining about my dad and saying how she wished she hadn't married him. I love my dad a lot, so I said, "Then I guess you wish I hadn't been born." My mom didn't say anything—which sometimes speaks for itself.

Leigh, age 16

Darrin came to live with our family after a failed suicide attempt. He was a nineteen-year-old young man who desperately needed encouragement. He is one of the most talented young men I've ever met. He's enthusiastic, smart, gifted in speaking, fun, and kind. Yet he had come to a point where he had given up on life. It wasn't easy those first few months. He had fallen into a pattern of self-destruction. Suicide is not the only way to destroy a life. Others can chisel away the spirit of a person through lack of encouragement. Darrin had given up on himself.

I feel like my mother made me feel stupid when I was weak in my faith and went to her for support. Now I see that maybe she could have been more supportive and less confrontational. My life was complicated, and I needed compassion through her faith in God.

Annie T., age 18

In the beginning Darrin countered words of encouragement from us with denial. Along with his family, his friends, and his pastor, we let Darrin know that his life was of value. In time, he began to embrace our words and accept them as truth. It was amazing to watch as God healed Darrin, scraping away his self-image of failure and replacing it with the knowledge that he was loved by God and by others.

My parents have always emphasized that I am special for three reasons: 1) I am a Christian; 2) I have a mother and father who love me no matter what; 3) When I grow up I can be anything that I want to be. When parents constantly tell you how much you mean to them and how special you are, you have a greater respect for them and for yourself.

Rachel K., age 18

Darrin is married now to a godly, beautiful woman and expecting his first child. He ministers to college students and shares his story of hope with others. He has grown into the man that he was intended to be from the beginning. A little encouragement can go a long way.

Mistake #4—Fights Are Always Bad

Question: Do you ever fight with your parents?

Yes! Doesn't every teenager?
Elizabeth H., age 14

Even in the healthiest relationships, people who love each other will disagree. All the teens I surveyed said that they fought with their parents at one time or another. Yet there is a difference between continual fighting and working through conflict. Fighting and petty bickering can cause deep rifts between you and your teen, especially when nothing is resolved.

Every now and then we fight about stupid, petty things. It's a mixture of both of our faults. I'm stubborn, and they don't like to compromise—not a good mix!
Kim Z., age 18

Continual fighting can not only damage the relationship between you and your teen; it can injure other relationships in the family as well.

I fight more with my mom than my dad. My mom and I are very different, so something may trigger her, and then something completely different will trigger me. Generally both of us get triggered, because we both think we're right, so we never give in until we just stop talking or my dad says that he's not choosing a side. Then my mom gets mad because he's not on her side and she drops it.
Kayla T., age 15

HOW TO HAVE A GOOD FIGHT

It would impact my faith if my parents looked at the big picture, not only the small things that I do.

Ben N., age 14

A good fight involves taking steps to resolve conflict. A good fight involves working through problems or disagreements and coming up with a workable solution, compromise, or plan of action. For those of you who have experienced the pain of fighting with your teens, a good fight might not even seem possible. Let me assure you that it is not only possible, but it is a positive way to strengthen relationships within your family.

I used to fight with my mom until we learned to communicate better. She realized I was different than her. Fights now are rare.

Sarah H., age 15

A good fight is determined from the very beginning. It's planned. It doesn't happen when tempers are hot and flared. A good fight occurs at a predestined time and place. It happens when you reaffirm the love that you have for one another before addressing the issues. A good fight means that you will both have the freedom to talk about things that are important to you. Each agrees not to say anything that is mean or derogatory.

My father always taught us that it takes two to have an argument. So no matter how bad you want to retaliate, just stay calm and quiet and walk away when the other is done yelling. Then take some time for both of you to cool down and talk over the matter. My father lived his advice.

Lacynda B., age 20

A good fight must involve good listeners in which each agrees to leave out personal accusations. Rather than pointing out individual flaws (such as "You're a slob"), you and your teen agree to discuss practical solutions (such as "I want your room picked up twice a week. What days are best for you?").

I think it's healthy to fight. We all take responsibility in the end.
Georgia P., age 16

My son and I are both passionate. My temper simmers, while his erupts. We both care deeply about issues. Once we came to an impasse and I determined it was time for a good fight. We had experienced a terrible confrontation the day before. I lost it. He lost it. Nothing was resolved. We were both hurt and angry.

I met with him in our front yard. We live on a small farm, and it was beautiful outside that time of the year. The pond was full, and the air was light and breezy. As we stood outside, it was peaceful. We were both wary in the beginning. I let Ryan know that I loved him and that I had said some things the day before that I regretted deeply. He responded and said that he had done the same. I told him that I wanted to hear what he had to say but asked that he listen to my side as well. I promised that we would try to work together to come up with answers. For the next hour we talked. I reaffirmed the positive things that he did. He said that he really needed to hear that from me. I listened as he shared frustration over some things that were happening in his life. I explained to him how much it hurt when he got angry over little things and how helpless I felt when I had no clue what was wrong. I asked him to let me know when he was hurting so that I could pray for him and encourage him. He gave me a huge hug and let me know that he loved me. The angry words from the day before dissipated as we sat on the tailgate of the truck and talked. It was the best fight we ever had.

We argue, but we don't really fight. Is there a difference?

Brianna B., age 16

Too often, fights are flashes of anger that burn up any hope of true communication. When your blood pressure is shooting through the top of your skull, it is not the best time to fight.

My mom is not always nice with her words, and I really let that affect how I feel about myself.

Annie T., age 18

It's better to walk away, letting your teen know that you will talk with her when you've both cooled down, rather than waste precious time and breath as you blast a hole in your relationship with angry outbursts.

My parents and I fight nearly every day. At least when we fight it means that I don't have to let them get close to me.

Eleanor T., age 16

Bickering and continual fights alienate you from your teen. It leaves a gap between you that seems impossible to close. But, when you work through conflict, you have an opportunity to see the situation from your teen's points of view.

I wish that my parents would understand where I am coming from and the stress I am under. I wish that they would hear me out before they begin to contradict what I am saying.

Becky S., age 18

So many parents are afraid that if they work through

conflict instead of laying down the law they will lose their authority. Let me tell you something: When you are out of control and your relationship is brought to a low of screaming and fighting, or if you must use physical force to make your teen bend to your will, you've lost your authority already.

When we fight, I just wish it would be handled through love.
Jessica L., age 14

At this stage of your relationship, your teen's obedience to your authority is based upon respect. When my son was a senior in high school, he was 6' 3" and weighed 190 pounds. I'm 5' 7" and—well, I'm not going to tell you my weight! The point is that he towered over me and I couldn't force him to do something that he didn't want to do. When I told him to do something, his obedience (and I expected it) was out of love and respect. That doesn't happen when I try to be my teen's friend. It doesn't happen if I ignore the problem and hope it goes away. It won't happen if I just give up because it's easier to let him have his way. All teens need structure, and it's our job to provide that structure through boundaries and consistent training, including reasonable consequences and encouragement.

I wish my mother would listen when I try to stop a heated discussion by saying, "Why don't we pray about it and try to talk it over tomorrow?" She tells me that I am using God as an excuse to get out of the discussion, and that hurts me to be accused of such. I wish God's Word and discussion of him was more prevalent in my household than it is, but that starts with individuals, not an entire family at once.

Lacynda B., age 20

Respect is earned when you treat your teen as you want to be treated. Wouldn't it be great if the Golden Rule applied to every other person except those who live under your roof?

My parents don't listen to what I have to say, as if I were still a little kid whose opinions don't matter.

Helen V., age 16

Well, the Golden Rule does apply to everyone who lives under your roof. Respect for others builds trust. When the Golden Rule is lived out, your teen knows what to expect from you. It's not a roll of the dice every time a conflict comes up. Will it be the good dad who wants to talk and show me the right way? Or will it be the dad whose head spins around while piercing, ugly words flow out of his mouth and into my soul?

I just wish we could end fights without being mad at each other. I really hate fighting with my dad.

Ashley B., age 14

I can hear parents grinding their teeth. "You don't know my teen!" you think. You're right; I don't. But let me bring you back to a foundational truth: The only person you can change is you. When you decide to work through conflict with respect, hope, dignity, and love, chances are your teen will respond.

Sometimes we have debates over little things that don't hinder our relationship but only enhance it. We need to know what each other believes and why.

Keith J., age 21

Mistake #5—You Won't Forgive and Forget

I would hope that they would actually care about helping and not tell me what I already knew was wrong.

Troy M., age 18

Once you resolve a problem, it's time to forgive and forget. If God puts our transgressions out of his mind as far as the east is from the west, why can't we forget about the mistakes that our teens made a year ago?

Just pray for me. When they always bring up how I messed up, it makes it hard. When I make a mistake, I know it. It hurts when they keep bringing it up.

Tracy J., age 15

We were leading a cell group in which one parent shared her dilemma. Her son had made a major mistake and was grounded. He was repentant in the beginning, but their relationship was starting to deteriorate. "I don't know what to do," the mother said. "He's angry all the time." We went through the events leading up to the present problem. How did they deal with his mistake? Did they talk about it? Had they set consequences? Her answers showed that they had taken positive steps with their son. Then I asked her how long he was grounded. "Indefinitely," she replied. "He's grounded until we know that he won't do this again."

Suddenly it was clear. There was no relief on the horizon for him. His punishment was not based just upon his actual mistake, but on all possible future mistakes. A punishment based on possibilities could last forever! He had been handed a sentence with no hope of parole, even in the face of good behavior. Consequences must have a beginning and an end. Teens must feel as if there is a chance for redemption. Once they break your trust, they want a chance to earn it back. When a punishment is ended, so is the event. They've served their time and now they have a chance to start fresh.

My parents forget that I do realize that I make mistakes and when I do mess up it is me who suffers the consequences. They feel obligated to show me every bruise and scar and wound on my heart, as if I didn't already know it was there.

Lacynda G., age 20

A fresh start can't happen if we continue to remind our teens of past deeds long after they've paid the consequences. The reminders of their failures hang over their heads, ready to crash down upon them at any moment.

My parents don't trust me because of my past. But in the past year I have not got into any trouble. I have earnestly tried to gain their trust, but no matter what I do, I can't!

Elizabeth B., age 17

When Blake was younger he made some serious mistakes and his parents had every right to distrust him. That was three years ago. Today he is a junior in high school, and he loves God. He's doing great in school. He is a leader in his youth group. He's planning on going to Bible school and entering the ministry one day. Yet there are times when he wants to give up. "If I don't clean my room, my mom reminds me that I'm a Christian. Then she goes off about how I've failed her in the past. It's discouraging. I want them to see me for who I am now. If I leave my stuff on the floor, then let's talk about that, but don't bring up my past!"

I told my mom about a mistake I made that almost destroyed my life. She was really great about it, but then she threw it back in my face later.

Annie T., age 18

A while ago I ran into some friends from high school. They made several references to how skinny I once was and reminisced about how shy I had been. They didn't mean any harm, and I didn't take offense. It was funny, because I could clearly see the confident woman that God has allowed me to become; yet as the night went on I remembered what it felt like to be the shy, insecure girl I was twenty-five years ago. My old friends had an image of a young sixteen-year-old teen in their minds and failed to see the woman sitting right in front of them. When we continually bring up our teens' past mistakes, we pin them down. We fail to see what they can be. They become stuck in the past. Remember that the past is gone. Allow your teen to take the steps necessary to learn from his mistakes and leave them behind.

I find it hard to tell my parents when I have had a revelation from God in my life, because I'm afraid that they won't see the change in me that comes from God or that they'll remember my past.

Anna A., age 15

We Won't Have All the Answers

I'm really struggling right now. I guess to help me, they could just love me and support me more. I need encouragement and the knowledge that no matter what happens they will support me.

Beth A., age 17

None of us has the right answers all the time. In fact, there are times when we don't know what to say or how to help. Sometimes our presence says more than words ever can.

When my son was fifteen years old, a drunk driver hurt him. I felt absolutely helpless. The drunk driver blacked out while driving seventy miles per hour and hit the car my son and his two friends were in. The drunk driver died on impact. My son—an all-around athlete—had twelve fractures from the waist down. He was in the hospital for six weeks and in physical rehabilitation for a year. One of my son's friends nearly died. He had twenty facial fractures and a punctured lung. The third boy missed serious harm when he was thrown from the vehicle. All of the families were left with a mountain of debt because the drunk driver lacked adequate insurance.

The accident and resulting consequences seemed so senseless. Ryan had to relearn how to walk. The doctors said that he would never be the athlete he once was. I had no clue how we were going to be able to pay the bills. I was torn because I felt sorry for the drunk driver's family even though he had wreaked havoc on our lives. The wreck could have been avoided, but a life had still been taken.

I prayed in the small bathroom of Ryan's hospital room. It was the only place that I could find to be alone with God. Though he had always been as close as a whisper, he now seemed a million miles away. I knew that God was faithful. Deep down I knew that he would somehow bring good from this bad situation. My head told me what I knew, but my heart was torn. Though I put up a strong façade for my son, I didn't feel strong.

One night an X-ray technician dropped my son when he grabbed the wrong sheets to lift him. This caused hours of agony, and the morphine couldn't touch Ryan's pain. I was by his side when my sister Mindy came to see me. She asked me to go home and rest. I couldn't leave my son. I hadn't eaten, so Mindy brought me food. Later that night I climbed onto the cot beside my son's bed, and my sister slipped in beside me. "If you're staying, I'm staying with you," she said. It was a tight fit as we squeezed side by side, but her presence was comforting.

That night Mindy never gave me one piece of advice, but she took turns getting up with me when Ryan's legs cramped. She rubbed my back and told me stories of our childhood that made me laugh. She gave me not one word of advice, but tangible acts that told me she cared. I don't think she knows what she did for me that night, but she made a painful situation bearable.

Parents can help when they try to understand more than trying to know it all.

Jeremy K., age 18

After several months of physical therapy, Ryan graduated from a wheelchair to a cane. He relearned how to walk and then run. The physical therapist released him for sports. Ryan signed up for track and attempted to run the 800-meter distance, a race he had easily accomplished the year before (he had even won the honor of going to state competition). I sat in the stands and watched him take his first lap, proud of the hours that he had worked and sweated and suffered to make it to this day. One runner after another passed him. Finally, I had to close my eyes after I watched him, his legs shaking with the effort, cross the finish line dead last. He collapsed on the grass and vomited.

Nothing I could say could give Ryan back what he had lost. I didn't want to embarrass him further by coddling him, but I couldn't stay in the stands while he heaved in the center of the stadium in full sight of all of his competitors. I made my way to him. His twin sister knelt beside him, her eyes filled with tears. "I am proud of you," I said. We walked out of the stadium to the car. My heart was heavy. Once again I struggled with feelings of helplessness.

We went to the physical therapist and asked some hard questions: Would Ryan ever run at a state level again? Would he be able to resume basketball the next spring? The answers were not what we had hoped. For the past year I had watched my son go through agony and yet keep a great attitude. He always had hope. He encouraged everyone around him. Now, for the first time, Ryan was angry. He pushed his way out of the office and climbed into the car, screaming in rage. "It's not fair, Mom," he said. "This is not fair!" He slammed his fist against the dashboard and wept as he gave up his dreams. I didn't offer false platitudes, because they would have been offensive. I told him that I knew that God had a plan for him. If it were in athletics, then we'd trust God together to take care of the details. But no matter what, we'd be there to support him. This is what Ryan had to say about that time in his life:

When I was hurt in the accident, my parents were there for me. It meant a lot to have all my family there the whole time, to know that I had someone at my back at all times. They thought positive the whole time, and that helped. It made me positive.

Ryan E., age 19

I never felt like I had the right answers to give Ryan. There were times when I felt less than upbeat, so it surprised me when he said that we were positive the whole time. He knew we were there for him, and that made it seem like a positive experience.

When our teens are in pain, they might not be looking for advice or words. They aren't looking for superheroes, just a human being who will reach out to them and care about the situation. Perhaps that is the one thing that has the potential to help them feel positive in negative circumstances. They may just need to know that someone is in their corner.

Going Deeper

Knowing that your presence can be a comfort can allow you to see your role in your teen's life. Understanding the mistakes that hinder conversation gives you the opportunity to take conversation with your teen to a deeper level.

I talk to my parents every day. I tell them the important things, the funny things, and the not-so-important things. We have a good relationship, so it [the conversation] often goes on to contemporary issues in faith, such as homosexuality.

Louise C., age 16

Talking with our teens is not one-dimensional. They have a lot to offer us. We can learn when they share their views on faith and the issues of the day. Sometimes when I talk with teens in small groups, I am amazed at the depth of their perception. I am the teacher, but they continually teach me. Talking with teens can give us a glimpse of the men or women that they are becoming.

Talk to me more and ask me more questions. Tell me more about your testimony and where you came from. Tell me all that God has done for you and how he has changed you. Let me learn from your mistakes and not have to make them again because you never told me about them.

Melissa A., age 18

Deeper conversations allow teens to get to know you as well, to hear what you think and to allow you to share ideas. One of the best rewards of conversing with your teens is being comfortable in conversation enough to laugh and be playful together. Developing strong communication skills will take work and time, but the gift received is the ability to see each other in a whole new light—not just as mom or dad, son or daughter, teen or adult, but as people.

I want my parents to have a true desire to know me. Not just, "How was your day?" but, "How is the problem you mentioned the other day? How's your Spanish class going? Your best friend? What can I help you with?"

Sarah C., age 19

Make It Real

A Love Note

Sometimes it's easier to write it than to say it. Leave a note of encouragement where your teen will find it. Let him know that you love him. Mention one positive thing that you noticed about him that week. Make the note brief.

Helpful Resource

The Five Love Languages of Teenagers by Gary Chapman (Northfield Publishing)—Discover your teen's primary love language and connect with her on that level. This book contains practical helps to determine how to reach your teen in a way that makes sense to her.

Tips to Effective Communication

Listen and let him talk.
Once she confides in you, never pass up an opportunity to keep your mouth shut.
Validate her worth to God and to you.
Encourage him with sincere praise.

Yelling is never a healthy option.
Offer advice in small doses.
Uplift your teen in prayer.
Remember to forget the past.

Transparency—be real. Your teen wants a human, not a superhero.
Expect great things—dare to believe!
Every parent should choose his or her words wisely.
Nothing worthwhile is ever easy; don't give up.

READY FOR A GOOD FIGHT?

What is the real issue?

What do you hope to accomplish? Write down up to three specific things that you hope your teen will understand when the conversation is ended.

____________________ ____________________

____

Write down two or three specific actions that your teen can take. Leave out any "you always" or "you never" statements.

Write down one positive thing that your teen has done recently. Affirm your teen by sharing that positive trait or action.

Reserve a time for you and your teen to talk.

Remember that conflict resolution does not occur in the heat of the moment.

Chapter Five

Show, Not Tell

I've learned that you can never be too old
to hold your father's hand.

—Anonymous 4th grader

Question: Do your parents teach you by showing you the "don'ts" or the "dos"?

I really just need encouragement. They are quick to tell me what I did wrong and punish me, but I rarely get encouragement or guidance. I'm just expected to do what is right.

Becca A., age 15

Our oldest daughter is only nineteen months older than the twins, so they passed all the big hurdles—driving, dating, and leaving home and college—at nearly the same time. I thought changing diapers for three babies was hard, but teaching three teenagers how to drive was insane!

When Leslie received her driver's permit, my husband and I took turns teaching her how to drive. We realized quickly that this would be a bigger challenge than we had imagined. She had an annoying habit of throwing her hands off the steering wheel when she panicked, and she pulled out of parking lots into traffic without looking because there weren't any stop signs. By the end of her first year driving, her older compact vehicle looked like a bumper car with all its dings and dents. She had backed into a car and several trashcans as well as spun around on a gravel road and hit an electric pole. She had even bumped into a man who was mowing the ditch in front of his property. When I asked her why she didn't stop, she said that she thought he would move.

We quickly came to the conclusion that our straight-A, lawyer-to-be, beautiful daughter was a bad driver. One night we were in the car (she was in the driver's seat, but it was still a joint effort at that point) and heard a siren. Leslie tightly gripped the steering wheel. "What should I do?" she asked. I glanced at her hands and noticed that they still clutched the steering wheel. We were making progress!

"Pull over to the side of the road and let the ambulance go by," I said. When the ambulance came into sight, Leslie swerved to the curb. But she didn't stop there. She then ran over the curb and sped into the nearby parking lot. A utility pole loomed before us. "Leslie, stop," I said, hoping not to alarm her but praying that she would get the message. It didn't work. She threw her hands off of the steering wheel and pulled her foot off of the gas pedal. The car was a standard and came to an abrupt, screeching halt. The seatbelts pinned us both against the seats. We stared at the light pole only one inch in front of the hood of the car. I slipped off my safety belt and took a deep breath as Leslie did the same. Without a word, we both climbed out of the car and traded places.

Understand that I'm young and that I learn as I'm growing up.
Kayla T., age 15

Adults Under Construction

Our teens are taking steps to become adults. It's our responsibility and privilege as adults and parents to show them the way. Teens learn as we patiently work beside them to help them take the reins of their own lives. This learning process is a partnership between teens and parents as we share with them how to assume responsibility, make life decisions, and learn practical skills.

Please say it in a way that I can understand.
Jennifer H., age 16

Too often adults toss out the "don'ts" and consider that to be a sufficient education. We tell our teens all the things that they should avoid—don't have sex; don't cheat; don't dress like that; don't talk like that; don't drink; don't do drugs—yet fail to show them what they *can* do and how to accomplish it. This also applies to faith. How many sermons are preached about what not to do while a teen is sitting in the pew wondering how to live his faith in a real world?

Everything that parents are against us doing, they connect with what God says. Sometimes I wish they wouldn't preach at me so much.

Kemis L., age 17

It would have been easier to tell Leslie all the things that she shouldn't do as a driver and walk away, but it would have also been dangerous. She needed us beside her in the beginning. If I had tossed her the keys and given her a long list of don'ts—don't tailgate; don't use your cell phone while you drive; don't get in a wreck—it would have been irresponsible of me. Yet it happens all the time with other issues in our teens' lives.

It was the "dos" that made Leslie a skilled driver—eventually. I showed her the basics—how to turn the key, how to use the brake, how to navigate in traffic. Then we graduated to the more difficult aspects—how to drive on slick or icy roads, how to merge in seventy-mile-an-hour traffic, what to do in case the car broke down on the side of the road.

They often tell me not to get into a position, but don't tell me how to get out of it once I'm in it.

Grace B., age 13

When our kids turn thirteen, we are showing them the basics—how to view themselves as God sees them, how to say no to temptation by making good choices, how to make friends that will treat you like a friend. By the time they reach sixteen we are somewhat in the passenger seat as we show them how to gain our trust by giving them greater freedoms (as they show that they are trustworthy)—how to choose a person of the opposite sex based upon something other than appearance, how to work to make and save money, how to look beyond high school and make goals for the future. By their senior years in high school they should be independent enough to take care of themselves. They should know how to do their own laundry, cook a meal, balance a checkbook, and have a work ethic, and they should have at least an idea of what they want to do with the rest of their lives. Spiritually, they are on the highway of life. You are an influence, but they are now making the calls. By this time, your teen is developing a strong personal faith and belief system that might or might not mimic yours.

Richard and I taught a college and career class for three years. We created a life skills class within that first year because many of the young adults didn't have the everyday skills they needed, such as how to change a flat tire, fill out a resume, or even write a check. It was clear which of those students had adults that invested in their lives and which did not. Spiritually, these young adults were making every critical decision in their lives—relationships, what God wanted them to do as a career, living their faith without any support—and the "don'ts" were not enough.

Many of those young adults hadn't received what they needed when they were thirteen, so at twenty years old they were trying to live independently without the foundational spiritual tools they needed. They wanted to know how to have a strong personal relationship with God. They wanted to understand how to discipline themselves to read the Bible and pray. Some of them were learning by trial and error.

They were still adults under construction, though they were adults in terms of age.

I want my parents to teach me by example.
Helen V., age 16

Growth Opportunities

Question: If you mess up, is there anything your parents can do to help you get back on track?

They can be forgiving and understand that I know I messed up and that I'm beating myself up enough for it. I don't need them to tell me what I did wrong or why it was wrong. Rather, I need them to be open, honest, and realistic.
Jenny M., age 19

When Leslie jumped the curb and almost hit the pole, she made a huge mistake—one that could have cost both our lives. But if she was going to learn to drive safely, it was my job to hang in there until she got it right. I couldn't give up because it was tough or because she wasn't grasping the fundamentals as quickly as I thought she should. Leslie is now a twenty-two-year-old senior in college, and she's a really great driver. In fact, she's been a good driver for five of the last six years. Her green Mustang has no dings or dents. She's on her way to law school, proving what we knew all along: A teen can be brilliant, but she still needs parents for some things. The five gray hairs I acquired during her driving lessons are my badge of honor. Though we love to tell stories about Leslie's early driving days, we have to acknowledge that those days are long gone and she is now an excellent driver.

My dad tells me that he never remembers a single time I have messed up. He thinks like I do. Mess up, forget, get up, and move on.

Georgia P., age 17

Your teen will make mistakes. Mistakes are growth opportunities. They give you a chance to show your teen how to take responsibility for his mistakes, work his way through them, and learn from them.

There are two extremes in parenting methods in our society. One is to protect a teen from the consequences of his actions at all costs. These are the parents who clean up the bathroom floor after their children even though they've asked them to put their dirty laundry in the hamper. They are the ones who assume the teacher is always wrong when it comes to their "baby" even though the "baby" is six feet tall with a goatee and this is his third violation. These parents are the ones who buy their teens new cars when they wreck the first ones or who talk to an influential friend at the court when their daughters are picked up on a DUI. This method of parenting sows irresponsibility in a teen's character. It stunts his or her maturity. It's not a gift to your teen.

They can avoid yelling. Discipline me in a way that I will actually be sorry for what I did. When my parents ask me to tell them something, they can actually listen all the way through and give advice, not criticism (there is a difference). They can be a good example in all they do and not put me down.

Linda S., age 14

Then there are those parents who don't bail out their teens when they make mistakes. Maturity is a direct result of growing through successes and mistakes. Responsibility is carved in a teen's character when he learns from his errors. Parents have the wisdom and experience to share ideas on how to make better choices the next time. They can set boundaries and consequences for their teens' actions. They can let their teens know that they will never give up on them and that they believe that they can and will do better next time.

I am struggling a lot right now. I don't think there is much my parents can do. To help me right now, they could just love me and support me more. I need encouragement and the knowledge that no matter what happens they will support me. I also think that they need to let me decide whether or not I really want to live the Christian life. I am at the age where I have to figure why I believe what I believe. I can't just take their word for it anymore.

Beth H., age 17

This second parenting method is extremely difficult if your teen is making choices that are not only damaging him, but also creating chaos and harming his relationship with your family. It's difficult when your teen is not living according to biblical principles. There is a heaviness of heart that only parents understand when you watch your teen reject what you know is right. It's the easiest time to simply walk away, but it's also when our teens need us the most. It's a balancing act as parents set boundaries and consequences and still determine to believe that God has marked their children with purpose.

I'm not struggling right now, but if I were I'd need them to be sensitive to what I was dealing with. I'd need them to reach out to help me, which may or may not include being talked "at." I'd need them to listen and talk to me and to work with me through whatever was going on. I would need them to love me no matter what stupid thing I had done.

Amanda B., age 18

Consistency

The key factor in the parent-teen relationship is consistency. Trust is developed between a parent and a teen when each knows what to expect. It happens when parents are true to their word and when decisions are not made in anger, haste, or fatigue, but upon the pre-agreed family guidelines. Those guidelines are not chiseled in stone but are in place so that everybody has a clear definition of what is expected in normal circumstances.

I just wish that they would be consistent. That is very important. Being consistent means praying with your children and caring enough to deal with every issue in a Christian way. Being a good example in every sense.

Annie T., age 18

Consistency occurs when teens understand that their parents are in agreement with one another. Decisions that affect our teens ought to be weighed and made behind closed doors. Teens might not see the compromise and decision making that went on between their parents, but they will recognize the strength and stability of two people in agreement who both want the best for their teen.

Helping Your Teen Get Back on Track

My parents raised me in a very loving environment my whole life. They don't put up with sin, but they are understanding and always have a listening ear and provide comfort. They are not overly strict. When parents are overly strict, that's when the teens feel too controlled and are likely to rebel. They are just strict about the important things. I'm glad that my dad puts his foot down. Love does not let the other person fall. If I was allowed to do just what I wanted, I don't know where I would be today. Sometimes you need someone to help you screw your head on straight.

Michelle H., age 17

When I was writing my first book, I interviewed hundreds of teens who were in bad situations—whether from personal decisions or from factors completely out of their control. Chad was one of the teens I interviewed. He was raised in a loving, godly home, but he began to drink in high school. He was a weekend partier, and by his junior year drinking was no longer a way to have fun, but an alcohol addiction. Chad's mom and dad weren't blind to what was happening. He consistently broke the rules, and they consistently enforced them, leveling consequences, making sure that he took responsibility for his actions. They loved him unconditionally, though he made their lives almost unbearable at times. They prayed for him daily, though it seemed the heavens were closed to them.

Encourage me. Let me know that, whatever it is that I'm going through, you will be there.

Pete D., age 18

[illegible]e night Chad left a party drunk. He stumbled, fell to the ground, vomited, and couldn't get up. He lay there in the mess and looked at his life, wondering how he had gotten there. He called out to God and turned his life over to the Lord. It was a pivotal moment. He went home and asked for help. Chad checked into Teen Challenge (a Christian organization for teens with life-controlling problems), and as a result he was completely changed.

They can talk to me, pray for me, and give me advice.

Jennifer H., age 20

As I wrote Chad's story, I thought about the mom who was at home praying for her son and trying to trust in God, even though it appeared that God wasn't listening to her. Although she couldn't see it, behind the scenes God was doing a work in her son's life. When the time came that Chad ran out of options, he turned to God for answers. It has been four years since that night. Now Chad is traveling with a youth mission team all over the world. He has a heart for the lost. He's an awesome young man with a powerful testimony of a merciful God and a mother who didn't give up on him.

I think they should encourage you to keep trying to find your way. Parents can't determine your faith for you. If you are having problems with your faith, it is between you and God.

April W., age 14

Chad's mom couldn't make him choose God, but she could pray. Chad said that even though he had given up on himself, he knew that God hadn't given up on him because his mom hadn't. That's a powerful statement. Chad's story, and hundreds of others like it, changed me as a mom and as someone who speaks and works with teens. No matter how bad the situation appears, I hear Chad's voice saying, "Don't give up on me." I now see teens in the light of a heart that longs for God, no matter what the actions or circumstances say to the contrary.

My parents can understand that we all mess up, forgive me, and help me to work through it with God and myself, rather than yell at me. Be there for me—really be there.

Katie P., age 17

We must allow our teens the luxury of learning from their mistakes, while at the same time believing in them and in the power of God. We can't continually bail them out, but we can set reasonable boundaries based upon their behavior and trustworthiness. We can consistently carry out the consequences when they go outside of those boundaries. Yet we must never give up on them. We must show them that they are loved—even when they seem unlovable.

They could explain that things in life aren't so bad, that everyone messes up every once in a while. They could give some examples.

Sam B., age 20

LETTING GO

They don't tell me what to do, and that has made me strong and independent, but they do show me, and that has also made me strong and independent. Actions speak way louder than words.

Melissa A., age 18

Are you a verbal list-maker? Do you teach your teen by him the things to avoid or not to do? Or do you put on your spiritual seatbelt and go for the ride, showing the way through your example or by giving him solid answers about why he should say no? As your teen learns, do you ease out of the way and let her hit the road on her own?

I was taught responsibility and about consequences at a young age. My parents don't really have to teach me about things that often now.

Steven S., age 16

Have you instilled confidence in your teen by giving her the tools she needs to make right decisions? Are you showing her the practical skills she needs as a young adult? Does he understand the family guidelines? Do you set reasonable boundaries and consequences? What about your teen's spiritual life? Have you shared steps on how to build a personal relationship with God? Do you live your faith? Does your teen understand that you love God and see a real relationship in your life with him? Rather than giving your teen a list of "don'ts," teach him to prosper spiritually, emotionally, and physically.

The first time Leslie drove alone on ice I followed her to school. I had showed her how to tap the brakes to grip the ice and how to watch for black patches. However, I wasn't sure if she was truly ready, so I followed her at a safe distance. She pulled into the school parking lot and my fourteen-year-old twins looked back to see if I was still there. I guess they were hoping that I wouldn't follow them into the parking lot. I didn't. I drove away, confident that Leslie had the skills that she needed. Had I continued to follow her past that time, I would no longer be showing her the way. I would only be undermining her confidence. She had proven to me that she was capable. It was clearly time to let go of that part of our training and let her assume responsibility for that aspect of her life.

She still needed me in other areas, and we moved on. As a senior in college, she still calls me on occasion for advice or for a listening ear. But the confident, assured twenty-two-year-old woman who is my daughter has come a long way from that unsure girl who used to panic and throw her hands off the wheel. As your teen grasps the necessary skills and tools to make it on her own, you are promoted out of the passenger seat as she takes the wheel.

It always makes me feel like I come from a loving home when my parents support me. It helps me when they say, "I love you, and I know that you'll make the right decision."

Kim R., age 19

Make It Real

Parenting Spotlight

1. Shine the spotlight on one area where your teen is struggling.

---

2. What parenting methods were used to handle the situation in the past month?

   What have you taught by your example?

   Does she understand the "why" behind the guidelines?

   Did you show him age-appropriate skills?

   Were you encouraging? Did you notice what she did right?

   Once he learned the skill and proved that he was capable, did you let go?

   Are you praying for your teen in this area?

3. What about consistency? How did you rate in this area?

   Is your teen clear about the consequences for violating a family guideline?

   Are the consequences appropriate to the action, not overly severe or lax, but reasonable?

Does she know exactly when the consequences will end?

Did you present a united front with your spouse?

Were you calm, or did you yell or use physical force to emphasize your point?

Did you forgive and forget when it was complete?

Chapter Six

It's a Trust Issue

Men are respectable only as they respect.
—Ralph Waldo Emerson

Question: Do your parents trust you?

My father always tells me that he trusts my decisions, because I make them and I take responsibility for them and my actions. I feel that my parents can trust me. I don't know what I could do to break that trust. I have it because I let them know what I do.

Georgia P., age 17

The issue of trust was one of the most popular issues I encountered in the surveys and in small group discussions. Some teens felt that trust should be given automatically.

Others believed that trust was a privilege. Many teens expressed frustration because they had made mistakes in the past and trust now seemed elusive. These teens weren't sure how to prove to their parents that they had learned their lessons. All the teens expressed a desire to keep, gain, or reestablish trust between themselves and their parents.

I love my parents, but I want them to give me some freedom to make my own decisions.

Kemis L., age 17

There were several teens who felt defeated. They were trustworthy, but they had less freedom than friends or acquaintances who were not trustworthy. The parents of these teens tightened their grip when their children were old enough to ride in cars with friends, drive, or start dating. Many of the teens said they were cruising along with a huge trust factor until that time and were shocked when Mom or Dad applied the brakes.

I'm trustworthy, but I feel that they only trust me when I am alone, not with any of my peers.

Becky S., age 18

These teens felt helpless because their parents' restrictions had nothing to do with their actions and they were unsure how to be granted additional privileges. The lack of trust was based on their parents' fears: fear of drugs, fear of drunk drivers, fear of peer pressure, fear of guns, fear of premarital sex, and fear of their teens being hurt. The "what ifs" frightened the parents.

I wish my parents would realize that they have a daughter with high morals and standards, one who cares about her future and about doing God's will. They need to trust me more and let me know that they do. I wish I had more freedom. I wish my parents and family didn't get so scared about things.

Alicia V., age 15

One young woman named Nikki shared her story with me. When Nikki was fifteen, she worked all summer to raise funds for a youth mission trip. The trip would be well chaperoned and organized. They planned to travel overseas and help build a church as well as evangelize in schools across the area. Nikki was a leader in her youth group and felt as if she had a call of God on her life to be in ministry. This trip was to be her first taste of missions work. She worked hard for three months, holding bake sales, washing cars, and cleaning out neighborhood garages to raise her trip funds. When the day came to turn in the money, her parents held a family meeting. They told Nikki that they had prayed about it and felt that God was telling them that the trip was too dangerous. She couldn't go unless one of them went with her.

Nikki was overwhelmed with disappointment. It wasn't that she was ashamed of her parents, but no other parents were going unless they were youth staff or sponsors. And this hadn't been the first time God had "spoken" to her parents. Every single time that Nikki had tried to take a step of maturity in the past year, her parents had somehow pulled in the reins. Though Nikki felt incredible peace about the mission trip, her parents did not—and that was the final word. Nikki could take a parent along for the ride or stay at home.

Nikki didn't know how to fight both her parents and "God" on this decision. She wondered if she would ever be able to step out in faith on her own. She wondered why God never spoke to her about the same fears her parents had. She questioned the peace and excitement she had felt about the trip.

Nikki didn't go on the trip. She gave her raised funds to other youth and allowed them to use it for their trip expenses. The mission trip was a huge success. One of the most discouraging moments for Nikki was when the youth testified about their experiences as she sat in the audience. She heard them talk about how they had led people to Christ and grown bolder in their witness. They described how the trip had encouraged them to touch the lives of their friends at school.

As she shared her story with me, Nikki wiped away tears. She wasn't angry with her parents or jealous of the other teens. Her acceptance of her situation was apparent, but so was her despair.

Earned Trust

It's not unthinkable that our children will face temptations and difficult situations or make mistakes when they spread their wings to fly. However, when trust is taken away or never granted when it is due, it can cause frustration and even rebellion. It's hard for parents to know when to let go and when to be strict. We are responsible to teach and train our teens to make wise life choices, and we are aware of the temptations they will face. Yet our teens continually tug at us to let them make those decisions on their own. Being able to both teach them wisely and give them responsibility is just one more balancing act that parents must perform.

Sometimes I wish they would let me figure out things on my own. I mean, I understand that they want me to follow their rules, but it would make it easier if they could let me go some. I know exactly what they want me to be, and I know right from wrong. I'd just like to prove that I'm strong enough in my faith to make the right choice instead of doing it because that's what they want me to do.

Katie H., age 15

When my teens left for college, I had no choice but to trust their judgments. Though we talked every night, I only saw them once a month. They loved us and we were a part of their lives, but they didn't need us to help them make decisions. They decided when to go to bed or if they wanted to stay up all hours. It was their choice to study and go to class. They made new friends that we didn't know. They went on dates with people we never met. If, and where, they went to church on Sunday mornings was their decision, not ours.

When I was younger, it was rare that I was trusted. If a parent never gives trust and then suddenly does, the child breaks loose and can really mess up.

Annie T., age 18

College can be a tough transition for many teens. If they have never been trusted and it is their first chance to spread their wings, they can free fall. If they've never learned how to make responsible decisions out of your sight, college life can be a brutal teacher.

If my parents could have changed one thing, I would ask them not to be so overprotective. I think it backfires when we go out into the real world. You are so naïve and you don't realize what is really happening around you. People can take advantage of you and your ignorance.

Brianne S., age 20

Independence is fostered in baby steps from the time that children are young teens. The purpose of these steps is to prepare them to leave home with all the necessary tools they need to function as young adults.

Anybody Got a Map?

If I could tell my mom or dad one thing and they would listen, I would ask them why I have a curfew of 10:00 P.M. as a seventeen year old.

Rebecca C., age 17

When your teen is between the ages of sixteen and eighteen, you might feel like you are in brand-new territory and somebody forgot to give you the map. Should you treat your teen like a friend? As a child? As a young adult? How can you know when your teen vacillates from one to the other in a space of five minutes?

My parents let me have freedom until I do something to lose their trust.

Jenell E., age 16

When Leslie entered her late teens, she asked for a later curfew and additional freedoms. She put her hand on her hip and arched one eyebrow like only she could do, trying to get me to see the bigger picture. She explained how she was responsible and how it was time for us to allow her to grow as a young adult. She made perfect sense, but I wasn't sure how much freedom was too much. What if she made a mistake? And why couldn't she keep her room clean if she was an adult?

My mom told me that she would always trust me until she had a reason not to. It makes me do good things for her.

Lindsey C., age 15

I watched other mothers with their adult children, hoping to gain insight, but it only served to confuse me. Some parents took off all the boundaries and let their older teens run wild. Others smothered them, treating them like small children when they were old enough to have children of their own.

I am very trustworthy. If I come in late, I tell my mom and we talk about it. I would lie about something that they asked me to do for them. I don't hide my world from my parents. I just don't want to have to give every detail. It is a pain to tell my parents the name of everyone who went to youth group, to the party, or who was at school. I say "everyone," but they want to know who "everyone" is. They know all of my friends, and I don't see why I have to name them all every time.

Brianna B., age 16

There had to be a middle ground between letting my older teens run wild and keeping them on tight leashes. The only thing I knew for sure was that I didn't have all the answers. Sometimes I set boundaries because I was older and I could see beyond the obvious. Other times I said no because it was easier. I didn't get away with that one much.

As my teens matured I realized it was time to say yes a whole lot more—but how?

Pressure and Release

I want them to understand and not treat me too harsh, but not hold off on what I deserve. To support me and help me.

Ricky M., age 16

One of my best friends, Faith, is a horse trainer. She uses a training method called pressure and release. Faith leads an unbroken horse into the ring. She grips the rope in her hand and leads the horse around the pen. As the horse learns to pace himself, she lets out a little bit of rope at a time until it lies in her open palm. She tightens the rope if the horse threatens to break loose or do something that will cause Faith or the horse injury. This process can go on for days. Eventually the rope lies loose in the palm of Faith's hand as she uses voice commands. The horse has learned to obey, and there is mutual trust between the horse and its owner.

My parents trust me because I have showed a lot of responsibility my whole life.

Jeremy K., age 18

Once there is mutual trust, then it's time to release the horse into the arena. Faith uses a small bit in the horse's mouth. She holds the reins loosely. Every light touch is a signal to the horse telling him which direction to take. If a horse starts to run away or buck, she pulls on the reins and puts pressure on the horse's mouth. The moment he responds, she lets go of the pressure.

My mom seems to be always trying to catch me doing something wrong.

Grace B., age 13

An inexperienced rider might keep the reins tight the entire time. This confuses the horse. He is responding, but the pressure is still there. He's unsure of what to do to make it go away. If the pressure remains constant over a period of time, it will desensitize the horse's mouth and he won't recognize the signals. He will only recognize the pain.

I hope that they will understand me and be compassionate, but at the same time punish me, because otherwise I will never learn.

Jen W., age 15

Many owners train their horses the wrong way. Some try to break the horses with a whip and end up with a rebellious, dangerous horse or a skittish horse with a broken spirit. Others pamper their horses, allowing them to develop annoying and lazy habits. Neither of these types of horses is able to function well outside of the round pen. These horses are unpredictable and sometimes dangerous.

When I make a mistake we have long talks, and they usually give me some practical ideas about what I can do, and sometimes they set boundaries.

Bekah P., age 18

When Faith's training is complete, the horse is reconditioned to respond to a light and gentle touch. "It's not about authority, but about relationship," she says. "We have to learn to trust each other. The horse has to know what to expect from me. When we're through with the training process, we have a mutual understanding."

My parents are consistent in their expectations, rules, and consequences.

Becky S., age 18

When our children approach their teen years, the reins are tight. As they mature, we begin to release the pressure. Teens are allowed to make choices and have greater personal freedom—a step at a time—while we see how they handle the responsibility. If they use bad judgment, they lose the privilege. That's the pressure. The reaction to the bad judgment is not harsh or unjust punishment, yelling, or rejection. It's consistent, an expected consequence that is a part of family guidelines. Teens know in advance that if they abuse the freedoms, they lose the freedoms.

They can tell me what I did that was wrong and then help me solve my problem. If I do something bad more than once, I get something taken away. My parents don't believe in hitting your kids to make them understand.

Amy A., age 12

Once teens demonstrate that they are capable of handling privileges, the pressure is released and they enjoy independence. We continue to train them to prepare for the larger arenas that they will one day encounter—college, careers, and relationships—until the rope lies loosely in our hands. The responsibility of mature behavior shifts from the authoritarian roles of the parents to the teens' shoulders when they leave home. They now make the judgment calls that affect their lives and have the necessary skills to do so.

Peace Versus Peace of Mind

I would hope that they would be understanding and respect that I am growing up and should be able to make my own mistakes and learn from them. They are not always going to be with me, and I have to be able to learn to handle my problems without them.

Brianna B., age 16

I was visiting with a friend recently. Her daughter was thirteen years old and preparing for her first mission trip. "I just don't have peace about it," she said. "I know that she's responsible and she'll be with adults who will take care of her, but I'm not sure that she's ready."

"Has she expressed the fact that she's not prepared?" I asked.

The mother shook her head. "No, she's totally excited. But I should have peace about this, shouldn't I?"

I laughed. "Welcome to the teen years," I said. "For the next few years you will not be able to make decisions based solely upon your peace of mind."

I can see readers all over the nation hesitating now. You were with me until this very moment, but after reading that statement you are ready to move on to the next parenting book. Shouldn't we have total peace about our children's decisions?

It would impact my faith if my parents trusted the judgments that I make.

Hannah N., age 15

First, let's make a distinction. There is a deep abiding peace that remains stable no matter what the circumstances. Then there's peace of mind. Fears and doubts can disturb peace of mind. God promises us peace, but not peace of mind. As parents, we will face doubts, questions, and fears.

My daughter Melissa traveled to a foreign country in the middle of wartime to smuggle Bibles to persecuted Christians. She is currently in Bible college and training to become a missionary. I have total peace with her decision, but as she gets closer to her goal, there are times when I struggle with peace of mind. Who knew when I placed this blond-haired baby girl in my pastor's arms the day we dedicated her that God would ask me to give her up one day? We all realize the sacrifices involved in missions, especially in the area that she has chosen. She's wrestled with it, and we've talked for hours about it. Melissa was the child who said that she would never leave home (of course, she was only seven at the time). She planned to build a house next door and hang out with us forever. She talks with us every night on the phone. Yet, she's the one who is called to minister in a nation whose government is hostile to the gospel. She's the one who will live far away from family and the support of those who love her most.

What is my role in this? To not be dictated by peace of mind, but rather to rely on the peace that is in my daughter's heart. To have confidence in her decision and to trust that she is in God's hands. To be thankful that she listens to God and obeys his voice. Sometimes I have fear, but it is balanced by the overwhelming peace that comes from knowing that Melissa is embracing God's call upon her life.

They encourage me to seek God's will and to do what he would want. They rarely pretend to know what exactly God wants for me.

Sarah H., age 15

WHEN TRUST IS BROKEN

Question: Are you trustworthy?

I've not been a perfect kid, but don't expect me to be, because you weren't perfect either. Help me instead of yelling at me. It will help me a lot more in the long run. I know it might be hard to keep your cool all the time, but it would teach me more about sincere Christianity than yelling at me and taking [away] some privilege. Let me do some small things, and if I lose your trust, be honest enough with me to make me realize that I lost it. Sometimes we can be totally ignorant and not realize that in your book what we did was wrong and we lost your trust. Just let me know. Tell me you want me to gain it back.

Stan T., age 15

When trust is broken, a rebuilding process must occur. A parent's sense of security is shattered as she imagines what could happen due to poor judgment or reckless actions. She doesn't know if she can trust her teen to tell the truth. How can we restore trust when it is broken? The first decision a parent must make is whether the wrong actions were intentional and willful or a mistake.

MISTAKE OR INTENTIONAL ABUSE

My parents impact my faith when they forgive me when I make mistakes.

Anna A., age 15

Mistakes. We've all made them. When we clean up the mess left behind, we learn from our mistakes. However, there's a huge difference between a mistake and intentional abuse of the rules. Many parents view mistakes and intentional abuses in the same light and dispense the same punishment for both actions.

Let's look at two scenarios. First, a teen is roughhousing with his brother, grabs the football, fakes a pass, and then tosses the ball. The brother misses it. The football hits the lamp and knocks it to the floor. Was it intentional? No. Is there damage? Yes. The boys' motivations were not evil; they were careless. They made a mistake. What are the consequences? The lamp cost $45, and they are responsible for replacing it, as well as for cleaning up the mess. This teaches them a life lesson: Throwing a football in the house costs you cash that you could've spent on a nice shirt. Next time they might take the football to the backyard to play a game of toss.

In the second scenario, a teen breaks up with his girlfriend when he discovers she's dating someone else. He follows her to a friend's house. When she goes inside, he takes out a baseball bat and destroys the windows in her car. Was it intentional and willful? Yes. Was there damage? Yes. The cost is $650, court costs, and damage to his reputation. His motivation was revenge, and he acted in rage. The consequences levied must be much more stringent for intentional behavior as opposed to a mistake.

Although my parents have been strict with discipline and made me take responsibility for all my actions, I would never change the way I was raised. Too many friends and even strangers have commented on how well my parents have done in raising us.

Becky S., age 18

It's not about punishment. It's about discipline. Discipline is teaching self-control and responsibility. Discipline makes a teen a better person and teaches him to take responsibility for his actions.

A Rebellious Heart

If the parent sees any signs, she needs to intervene, because ultimately kids know it is wrong. They just want to do it anyway because they don't care. If parents will take a stand for their kids, in the long run the kids will thank them.

Michelle H., age 17

If a teen is in rebellion and making willful decisions or intentional actions regardless of family guidelines, then consequences and boundaries create the pressure needed to discipline him until he changes that behavior. Decisions about trust should never be made in the heat of the moment. Consequences are deserved, but so is love. A teen should never see disappointment in her failures as a lack of love for her as a person.

It's discouraging when our teens rebel not only against us, but also against God. We must be honest about the condition of their hearts. If they are not living their faith, then we acknowledge that. God doesn't make them serve him, and we can't make them, either. Being honest allows us to separate their actions from their faith or lack thereof. We cannot discipline them into serving God.

Being honest allows us to place our teens in God's hands. He loves them even more than we do, and he has a plan for their lives. We can pray for them. We can love and accept the people that they are, separating who they are from what they do. All the while we can allow them to take responsibility for their intentional or willful actions.

A Repentant Heart

I've learned to communicate these things to my parents, but it wasn't always like this. I've done tons of things like seeing movies my parents objected to or getting car rides with people that they didn't want me to hang out with. Now my parents trust me because they know I'm trustworthy.

Rebekah A., age 20

What do you do when your teen has made a 180 in her life? How do you know when to extend trust again? Christa bombed her junior year. She started to hang out with several girls who were popular. She felt special being in their group. She went to parties where alcohol was served, but she didn't drink. Yet the rule in her household was that she couldn't go to parties where underage drinking was involved.

Another family guideline was that everyone in the family would always be truthful. Christa wasn't always truthful. She started spending the night with her new friends. They snuck out, staying out all hours of the night. One night Christa met a guy at a party, and he offered her marijuana. That night she got high for the first time. Before long she was getting high every weekend. Eventually the police raided a party she attended. Her parents found out that she had been lying to them when they were called to the police station. They were devastated. They grounded Christa, took away her car, and explained that they loved her but could no longer trust her.

"At first I was mad, but then I realized what I had lost. My parents had always trusted me, especially my dad. He had always said how proud he was. When he was young he spent time in prison. He had a bad childhood, and he turned to drugs, alcohol, and crime. He was saved in jail and determined that his family would be different. He's always loved me and told me how proud he was that I had not made the same mistakes." Her dad's tears broke Christa.

If I ever did anything to hurt one of them emotionally, I would have a rough time. But I would tell them if I made a terrible mistake. I would want them to know that I care enough for them that I would be honest.

Teddi H., age 13

That night Christa apologized to her parents, and they prayed with her. She was truly repentant for her actions and ready to accept the consequences. When the grounding was over, Christa was ready to reclaim her parents' trust. Her father explained that it would take time to rebuild their trust. However, he assured her that it was definitely possible and that they would work together to make it happen.

Let me know when I have gained some of that trust back so that I know that in your eyes what I've done isn't completely bad and that you don't think that I'm a bad kid anymore.

Stan T., age 15

When teens damage the trust you have in them but offer repentant hearts, create a game plan with specific and reasonable steps so they know exactly what is expected of them. Share the plan with them so that they clearly understand that it is possible to regain your trust. As they make good choices, reward them through positive reinforcement such as encouragement and affirmation.

I did some pretty bad stuff that rightfully caused them to mistrust me, but I believe I've gained most of the trust back.

Ricky M., age 16

MAKE IT REAL

What Are Your Family Guidelines?

Work with your teen to create a list of family guidelines. Brainstorm. Discuss consequences that are appropriate. Create guidelines that are appropriate and reasonable for your family. Don't get bogged down in minute details.

Family guidelines are not to discourage family members or set impossible standards. They are to partner with each member of your family so that everyone has input and understands the expectations. The following are only examples.

Guideline	Consequence
Each family member will help with chores.	Additional chores
If a family member is late, he or she must call.	Loss of one privilege

We will always tell the truth to each other.	Loss of privileges
If you break or abuse someone's property, you replace it.	Work or pay for item

Note: I recently watched a television program where a mother had a list like this on every wall of the house. The lists were prohibitive, and some of the consequences were "toss the laundry on the front lawn" and "put red pepper under the tongue." These were not family guidelines but endless rules with unreasonable punishments. Family guidelines are not intended to frustrate but rather to help family members work together toward a set of common goals. Consequences should NEVER embarrass or alienate.

Prayer for Your Struggling Teen

Lord, I pray for ______________________. I ask that you soften his/her heart. Though _____________ is struggling, help me to love and believe in him/her just as you have believed in me.

Give me wisdom to deal with every situation. Help me to not take it personally when ________________ makes harmful decisions, but to be consistent as his/her parent in both love and discipline. When I am weary, help me to turn to you for strength and peace. When I am angry, help me to see my child through your eyes. Show me the possibilities that you see in ________________. Let each day be a new day as I forgive the trespasses of yesterday and start over with new hope.

Father, help me see the possibilities that you see in me as a parent. Help me to understand that I am not alone. Remind me that you are walking with me through this.

I pray that ____________ sees your love inside of me. Help me to be like Jesus to him/her, even when I don't feel like it. Thank you for your love for me. Thank you for your love for my child. Thank you that you have marked ______________________ with a special destiny. I will trust you and walk in your footsteps until I see your plan unfold in ___________'s life.

Chapter Seven

Home Sweet Home

There's no place like home. There's no place like home. There's no place like home.

—Dorothy, *The Wizard of Oz*

Question: Is your home a safe place? Why or why not?

My home is a safe place physically in that I am not abused. I'm fed, and I have the basic necessities. But a safe place in terms that I can act and be myself and be honest? No, not really.

Janelle T., age 15

Home is where you kick your shoes off at the door. It's where you are able to leave behind pretenses. It's the one place where you can be yourself. Home is an emotional shelter, a sanctuary from the stress of work, school, or life. It's where the people you love the best reside. Though it might not have the most expensive furniture or a kitchen that will grace the cover of *Home* magazine, it's comfortable and it's your domain.

Our house is so crazy. You never know who is going to just show up and hang out. There are five of us kids, and all of our friends can come over uninvited. Our house is very "kid friendly" and I think that is why so many people feel comfortable coming over.

Rachel K., age 18

The best part of any trip is coming home. I often travel in ministry. When I pull into my driveway and see my horses running in the pasture and my dog standing by the fence to greet me, something inside of me is at peace. I'm home. Inside the four walls of that modest home are the people that I love the most. Home is where I can sit in my favorite spot—a recliner where I tuck my O.U. blanket over my shoulders and read a favorite book. It's where I've made memories with my husband and children. It's truly home sweet home for me.

Yet home has not always felt this way for me. When I was growing up, home was a difficult place to be. I hated conflict, and yet I was surrounded by it. I was a peacemaker at heart and wasn't sure how to act or what to say to make things better. Sometimes I made things worse when I tried to intervene. Home definitely wasn't a place I wanted to share with my friends. I felt stuck at times because I was too young to leave. I wanted things to be different when I became an adult and had my own family.

Dude, no way will I ever be like my parents. My home will be so much different. It's not even funny! It would take forever to tell you everything I would like to do differently.

Mercy D., age 15

My childhood home wasn't bad all the time. There were moments when being at home was nice. My dad has a laugh like a cartoon character, and every time he laughed, we all got tickled. I played outside with neighborhood friends. I fished with my parents and siblings at Keystone Lake. It's just that when it was bad, it was really, really bad. Home was unstable. I never knew what to expect.

My best friend Kathy's house was much like mine, so I assumed every family had the same struggles. When I started attending church, I met a whole new set of friends. I was invited to spend the night with some of them, and I watched the interactions of their families as if studying a work of art. The canvas of their relationships was amazing! Deep inside I longed for the same thing. For the first time in my life, I realized that the things that went on inside the four walls of a home were very different from house to house.

I have written a letter to myself to remember when I raise a child to do things my mom didn't do.

Lara M., age 17

It's not fair, but it's reality. Some teens have a greater advantage—parents who love them, stability, homes that are safe from addiction or abuse, moms and dads whose marriages are intact. They have the confidence of knowing that there are people within shouting distance who believe in and support them. This doesn't mean that they have perfect lives or that they don't encounter hardships, but they have a place to go. These teens know they don't have to face the world alone.

Recently I was teaching on a Sunday morning and asked if any of the students had a prayer request. Jenny lifted her hand. "My mom left last night. We were alone until my grandmother could come get us. I want you to pray that Mom gets help." My heart sank. This was not the first time Jenny's mom had left. The silence in the room was tangible. That a mom would abandon her children was inconceivable to most of the teens. The differences in their worlds were striking.

At thirteen, Jenny is one of the youngest students in my discipleship class, yet she is well aware that people can fail her. She understands what it feels like to be abandoned. She has no clue what it feels like to have a consistent home life. If she did not have a loving grandmother, her chances of living her faith would be slim. Statistically, these abandoned girls are the ones who believe it when guys say that they love them because their need for love and acceptance is so great. These are the teens who struggle to believe that God really listens. It is hard for them to grasp the news that God is a father who will never leave them when their concept of a father figure is negative or abstract.

My grandma/guardian didn't say anything, but I was a monster when she and her husband took me into their home. It made her cry. I felt my heart break. This has made me want to make my life and who I am the best it can be. Until I was ten, my home was very unstable. Drugs, sex, abuse, and hunger surrounded me. Since then I have had a very good home life, and it is the only place where I can feel truly safe. My new parents tell me that they love me. They have never really fought or argued around me, and they are very good people.

Jenell E., age 16

Youth ministry programs often focus on influences such as sex, alcohol, friends, and music in an effort to touch the lives of teens. These are important issues, but the family home is more influential than any cultural influence. Every home environment affects the way that teens relate to people, shapes their problem resolution skills, and either nurtures or batters the children's self-esteems. The importance of family is why many youth ministries now reach out to the entire family, rather than just to youth. Youth ministries impact teens only two to three hours a week. If the home environment is in crisis, then that influence can easily be lost as a teen struggles to be strong in adverse circumstances.

Even in homes that do not struggle with abuse or addiction, teens have a wish list because home is so important to them. In a world where teens are tugged and pulled by outside influences, the home is their refuge. The following are five things that teens hope to find in the safety zone called home.

#1—A Home that Is Welcoming

My parents have always been hospitable. I really admire their hospitality. They are always ready to take someone in, whether it is for a night or for a year. They go out of their way to make others comfortable and are very selfless in doing so. I would like to be self-less and hospitable, even as a college student.

Lanae P., age 19

Have you ever walked into a home and immediately felt welcome? The environment was warm and inviting. The host put finishing touches on the meal or events of the night that made your time together special. The conversation was great. When you left, you looked forward to returning.

Have you ever walked into a house where the host or hostess was distracted? Perhaps he or she was impatient to get the night over. The meal was great, but the conversation was stilted. Have you ever felt like you were invited out of duty?

What is the environment in your house? Teens live in a society where acceptance is not easily given. It is vital that teens feel welcomed in their own home and by their own families. Busyness is often an excuse for dismissing hospitality at home. Many families have a lengthy list of things to accomplish. Parents often feel stressed or overwhelmed. The last thing most fatigued parents want to do is to give of themselves to one more person.

My family is a loving and caring family, and I want my friends to meet my parents.

Jennifer L., age 15

Hospitality to your teen is not about serving her every whim. It's not about serving gourmet meals. Hospitality can be experienced over a meal of chilidogs and in a household where give and take among family members is expected. It's less about action and more about attitude. Hospitality is about giving a part of yourself to family that is normally reserved only for company. It's allowing your teen to see your welcoming smile, to feel the extra touch that only you can give.

Have you ever watched your teen from a distance and marveled at her personality? The same somber, unexpressive teen that hibernates in her room with headphones blocking out all unnecessary family interaction comes alive around others. She's witty and fun, and her smile lights up the room. You can see why people are drawn to her. You wish that she would share that part of her personality with you.

Sometimes your teen sees the same thing in you. She watches as you smile and laugh with others, or how you go out of your way to make a difference—only to see that hospitality disappear once you are at home. Your family is just as deserving—actually, more so—of warmth, kindness, and generosity of spirit from you as are strangers, neighbors, or the kids in your Sunday school class.

Several years ago I was running late for church on a Sunday morning. I was cranky. It had taken forever to get everybody in the car, and I had only five minutes before class started. As I drove, I listed the infractions of the morning, explaining that next week everybody would have to do better. We zoomed into the parking lot, and I grabbed my Bible. My young children ran behind me as I race-walked down the hall. When I saw one of my students, I took a deep breath and smiled warmly. "How are you? I'm so glad to see you. I'm almost there. Tell everybody to sit tight. I'll be there as soon as I drop my children off at their class." I gave her a hug and continued down the hall. Five-year-old Ryan looked up at me with his big chocolate brown eyes and pierced my soul with his innocent words: "I wish I was in your Sunday school class, because you are really nice to them." Ouch!

I feel one hundred percent secure in my home, because when I'm feeling down I'm always lifted up. And when I feel like I need a hug or affection, it's always there.

Samuel B., age 20

As a Sunday school teacher, my ministry goal was to touch the lives of teens through love. I made it a point to give every teen an embrace and a smile. I wanted them to understand that their presence in my life, even for that moment, was a good thing. But my son's words were a powerful reminder that I had given my love and presence to a teen and denied my own children the same things just that morning. It was hypocritical to flip my Sunday morning mask over my face when I entered the doors of the church. This is one of the reasons so many Christian teens, especially those whose parents are in any type of ministry, become disillusioned. Hospitality must start at home.

My son's words never left me. I vowed from that day forward to do better, even when I was under pressure. I have failed at times, but it remains one of my main goals as a parent. I want to be real, but I want my teens to feel welcomed by me. I want them to see me laugh. I pray they glimpse the person that I am on the inside in addition to my mom side.

My home is the best place in the world.

Teddi H., age 13

Is your home a hospitable place for your teen? Does he know that you welcome his presence? This may be difficult when your child is less than cordial. If this is the case, remind your teen of your expectations on how to treat family members, but lead by your example. Show your teen the true meaning of hospitality.

My mother is so nice and generous and loving, so I hope to be those things.

Sarah C., age 19

#2—A Home Without Continual Conflict

My house is a safe place except for when my parents are mad at each other; then I'd rather be anywhere else but there.

Bekah P., age 18

A home is an environment in which conflict does not rule. Disagreements will arise in any home, but a safe atmosphere is one in which family members work through problems to find answers. Conflict resolution is an important part of your teen's development and maturity. She will use conflict resolution skills in future relationships, careers, and families.

My home is not a safe place. I am always worried that my dad will be in a bad mood or that I haven't done everything that they asked and get yelled at. My parents usually fight. My dad and I have our differences that we usually voice toward each other.

Elizabeth B., age 17

Is your home a battlefield? Are your children forced to listen to unresolved arguments and rehashed conversations? When fights are between parents, teens may hear the arguments but not be privy to the apologies or resolutions. When children see continual conflict without resolution, it spawns insecurity. Parents are the rock of their teens' worlds. Constant fighting and bickering only splinter that foundation.

The one thing my parents could do to impact my faith is to stop arguing and work out their differences more peacefully and Christ-like. Just being around an atmosphere of anger and arguing is hard to deal with, and it makes me angry with God for not doing something to stop it, but I know better now. I just wish they would stop.

Sarah A., age 15

There are also households where problems are not discussed even though they are clearly evident. This occurs where one member is making harmful or selfish choices and the entire family is affected. The underlying tension produces frustration in those who are helpless to change the situation. The illusion of family harmony may fool the world, but it doesn't fool our teens.

Many times, there will be arguments because my mother wants a Christian husband. He claims he is, and this causes chaos. This is an example of why Christ said to yoke with another believer. It takes away this aspect of tension.

Vickie M., age 21

Teens define a safe home as a calm, loving environment. Many teens stated that if they could change one thing about their home lives, it would be to eliminate yelling and petty arguments and to learn how to work through problems as a family.

Yelling is not the answer.

Annie T., age 18

One way to resolve conflict is to create a common set of shared values. If parents expect respect, then every member must show respect in their tones of voice and the words they speak to each other. If it's unacceptable to yell or get physical in a disagreement (and it always is), then make a guideline that conflicts will never be resolved in the heat of anger. Everybody agrees to retreat to a neutral part of the home and get back together in a couple of hours to discuss the issue when tempers have cooled.

I like the way we handle fights. We are alone for a little while and then apologize and go on with our lives.

Steve W., age 15

The reward of shared family values is that the entire family benefits. Your teens learn the value of working as a team to solve problems. They learn how to work through conflict with communication rather than outbursts. The entire family experiences the benefit of growing closer rather than pushing each member into a defensive corner.

#3—A HOME THAT IS OPEN TO FRIENDS

Question: Do you want your house to be a place where friends can come over?

I don't feel like I can bring my friends here without an invitation or just have them stop over if they have a problem. This is something that I was actually thinking about, and I was also thinking about it in terms of the church and my youth group and things. I feel that as a society, at least with my teenage friends, we feel as if everything has to be planned, in the bulletin, every one of our days and weeks planned. Nothing can be spontaneous anymore. This sort of goes along with my house.

Janelle T., age 15

Teens wrestle and bang into furniture. They are ravenous and always seem to pop in just as dinner is served. Teens long for a place to simply hang out. Is your house on their list? Do your teen's friends feel comfortable enough to drop by, or is your teen always at someone else's house? It's not easy to open your home to strangers, yet all but one of the teens surveyed said they wanted their homes to be a place where friends could come over. It was a deal breaker. These teens were willing to clean up before and after and to abide by rules in order for this to occur.

We have an unwritten rule in our household that our children can bring their friends home to spend the night without having to ask for permission. We implemented this when we realized our teens had a tougher curfew than many of their friends. Some of them had no curfew at all, even though they were in high school. We didn't want to change the curfew, because we felt it was reasonable, but we did want to give our children an alternative. Opening our home allowed them to continue to visit with their friends. We knew who they were with and where they were. It was a win-win situation. Teens enjoy having a place where they can have fun with friends, but it's not only the teens who benefit if that place is your home.

Why Is It Important?

I totally love that about my house! It's almost always okay for one of my friends to come over. Sometimes my mom even asks if I want to have people come over to watch a movie. This week we are having the youth group over, and it was her idea! My friends' parents are strict about having friends over, so we usually all hang out at my house. There are boundaries set, but they are sort of unwritten. We just know them without my mom having to say anything.

Laura N., age 15

Opening your home to your teen's friends is the number-one way to combat negative peer influence. I meet parents who are concerned that friends will influence their teens, yet they don't know their teens' friends on a personal basis. They vaguely know about them but know little about their families, their ambitions, or what they are like as people.

Opening your home shifts the power of influence from peers to you. When the teens are sitting in your living room and eating cookies at your kitchen table, you get to know them on a first-name basis. You have opportunities to talk with them—and perhaps even consider them friends of the family before long.

I always ask my mom, and she almost always says yes. So really, it is just a matter of taking into consideration what she thinks and if she really wants company. Yes, I would very much like my house to be a place where my friends can come.

Amber T., age 15

You set the tone for the night as teens have fun without making negative choices. Not all of your child's friends will be Christians. Many of them will be seekers. Just because one of your teen's friends attends church doesn't mean that he or she is living a life of faith. There are teens in churches all over the nation who attend because they are forced to, because youth group is fun, or because they want to meet a certain "hot" Christian guy or girl. Having your teen's friends in your home allows them to see Christianity in action. They see real people who are not perfect but who love God and each other. They see you when you mess up and when you make it right. Christianity gets on a level that they can understand. It is attainable.

Living your faith isn't confined to Sunday morning but is threaded throughout everything you do. It influences how you treat each other and what you allow in your home. Best of all, it encourages your teen's friends to consider the possibility of knowing God.

My house became a house where my friends would go when they had problems at home.

Serina-Linn C., age 16

Opening your home to your teen's friends may seem like a gift that you give to them, but it's definitely a gift to yourself, too. Knowing your teen's friends on a personal basis allows you to touch their lives and therefore to be a part of your teen's circle of influence.

BOUNDARIES

Question: Would you be willing to have boundaries if friends could come over?

I want my house to be a place where my friends can come, and I am quite willing to have boundaries.

Gemma M., age 13

Create guidelines concerning your teen's friends coming over that make sense with your schedules and family preferences. Make them reasonable so that having friends over is an enjoyable experience for the entire family. If you want your teen and his friends to sit quietly and visit, then the odds are they'll pick another place to hang out. However, it's not unreasonable to ask that they keep the noise to a comfortable level.

My daughter's friend Emily is loud, but she is also hilariously funny and talented and has a heart for God. We love having her in our home. She has made us laugh more than any other of our children's friends, but if it is late and we are trying to sleep, we sometimes have to gently remind our teens and Emily that the noise needs to come down a notch.

My home is a safe place and a fun one!
Sarah H., age 15

What are your fondest memories of childhood? Are they the pleasant smells of pine cleaner on your kitchen floor or that spotless utility room? Most likely, your fond memories have nothing to with an immaculate house, but with people, activities, and spontaneous moments.

One of our family's favorite memories concerns Melissa's friend April. She was notorious for leaving her clothes at our house. In fact, it appeared that she was slowly moving in, leaving one item at a time until her entire closet was stored at our house. Several of her white, oversized T-shirts, all with basketball or softball logos, eventually mixed in with our family's laundry. One day April came by as we were all eating breakfast. It was early morning, and we were all in T-shirts and shorts. She sat down, grabbed a plate, and then stared at us for a moment. "Hey!" she said, pointing her finger at all of us. We burst out in laughter when we realized that every one of us, including my son and husband, was wearing one of

April's T-shirts. I doubt that our home was immaculate at the time, but that didn't tarnish this memory—or several other good ones that involve our children's friends and our home.

My friends come over all the time. Everyone loves coming over to my house and thinks my parents are the best (I think that's just because they don't live with them). I like the fact that my friends always want to come over. It makes my house full of energy and fun. My parents do set up rules like "Clean up after yourself" and "If you're coming home late don't be too noisy," but that's understandable because there's usually nine of us over at a time.

Beth R., age 17

All teens will not share the same value system as your family. Their families may allow things that you do not. For example, our family doesn't watch movies with certain ratings, so this guideline applies to movies watched in our home by our teens and their friends. Our teens know to stay within the family guidelines, even if another teen sees nothing wrong with certain movies. We don't make a big moral issue out of it; it's just a simple expectation. If someone were to bring an R-rated movie to the house, our children would offer to go get another movie or select one of the several we have available at our home. I try to pick up a new video on occasion to have a good selection available. This way when the issue comes up there is no condemnation, no fuss, and no bother. They just select another movie and prepare to munch on popcorn and brownies and have fun!

Yes, I want my house to be a place where friends can come over, and I would be willing to have many boundaries for friends to come over.

Alicia V., age 15

As for food, we have a separate snack cabinet that is open to everybody. It has popcorn, cookies, Fruit Rollups®, and chips. Snacks don't have to be fancy. Teens appreciate the inexpensive box of snack cakes, even if we don't. When teens visit for the first time, we show them the cabinet and let them know that if they're hungry, they're free to grab a snack. We keep juice and soda on the top shelf of the refrigerator. If a teen drops by at suppertime and we have enough food, he is invited to eat with us. If we don't have enough food, I make him a sandwich or give him something to drink.

Let your teen know that you want your home to be open, but share the expected boundaries with them. Explain that they can't devour a week's worth of groceries in one night. Clarify that you expect your teen and her friends to tidy up any messes that are left. If friends don't help, let your teen take responsibility. After she cleans up by herself a few times, she'll ask her friends to lend a hand.

Oh, my gosh, my friends drop by all the time. My parents love to meet my friends. I had a small party the other night, and I cleaned the house all day long so that my mom and dad would let me. It seemed like nothing, because it was worth it to have my friends over.

Salena B., age 18

#4—A HOME THAT ISN'T PERFECT

I don't like having my mom stress over having the house clean, because she goes way over the top. This makes it hard to have people over. When I have kids, I won't be as uptight about things like having the house clean or making sure the cars look good. I'll work on having relationships with them more than freaking out over little things.

Katie H., age 15

If you want the house to be perfect before your teen's friends show up, then they might not ever come over. Can I share a secret with you? Most teens don't even notice if your house is less than perfect, but they will notice a home that is warm and inviting. Our children's friends might see folded laundry on the couch or a few dishes in the sink if they drop by without an invitation, but I've never had a teen refuse to come back because she was forced to view our clean clothes.

A house that is perfect makes a better museum than a home. It's pretty, but it's impossible to feel totally at ease in it. I visited a home once and was impressed by the organization and neatness. The yard looked like a park. The hostess proudly showed me through the home and outdoors. She even showed me the laundry room and opened closet doors! In my house, closets are privy only to family members and friends—really close friends.

At this home, when I set my glass down, it instantly disappeared. The children walked in from school, slipped their shoes off at the door, and immediately picked them up and took them to their rooms. I was excited to know that this could happen without the children being asked. I tripped over Ryan's size thirteens almost every day and had to remind him to put them in his closet. By the end of the hour at that house I was ready to offer myself as a student. I would sign up for any course that might teach me how to run such a tight ship. This was a perfect house!

Yet as time went on, I realized that the house was much less a home than it was a set of rules. Chore lists were neatly typed and in every room of the house. Detailed guidelines dictated mealtime, phone time, chores, laundry, and homework. No single detail was overlooked. Feet couldn't be placed on the ottoman because it might dirty the fabric. Food was restricted to mealtimes and could only be eaten at the kitchen table. There were pre-sliced veggies in the refrigerator; all other snacks were off-limits. Any smear, smudge, or imperfection was a big deal and immediately remedied. The teens were even instructed to walk with their feet spread apart when they walked down the hallway to avoid wearing a track in the middle of the carpet. Many of the rules made perfect sense (except for the carpet rule), but the house was so micromanaged that the comfort zone was eliminated.

A house with too many rules never feels like a home. If neatness is a high priority, set stricter guidelines for some rooms and relax them for another area like the family room. Let there be areas where it's okay to be imperfect. If you want your teen to eat healthy, let him select nourishing foods that he enjoys. It's all about compromise. This is not a lack of control but cooperation between family members to make a house a home.

I understand that they want me to follow their rules, but sometimes it would make it easier if they could let me go some.

Katie H., age 15

#5—A HOME WHERE YOU PLAY TOGETHER

When they were little, our children wrapped their arms around our necks and begged us to spend time with them, to have tea in tiny cups or to race miniature cars on the kitchen floor. Now they throw good-bye kisses to us as they walk out the door to spend time with friends. Due to conflicting schedules and varying interests, many families stop playing together when their children enter their teen years.

Playing together as a family is a great way to stay in tune with your teen. However, playing together means spending time together with no serious agendas. One cartoon I saw showed a father and son fishing. They were isolated in the middle of the lake when the father cleared his throat and said, "Son, about that sex talk we never had …" The son threw his hands up in the air and said, "Aha! I knew it!"

Me and my mom talk almost every night. She stays up late and waits for me to come home from class, and we chat. I bounce ideas off of her. My dad sets aside date nights for me.
Rebekah A., age 20

It's perfectly acceptable to spend time with your teen simply because you want to hang out with him. Though the fishing scenario was only a cartoon, I wondered how the son felt. He had risen before dawn, was sitting in a smelly boat and placing slimy worms on a hook—all because he thought his father wanted to spend time with him. I'm guessing that in real life this teen would feel cheated. There are times when you will spend time with your teen to talk about issues, but real intimacy is developed when you make time for your teen for no other reason than that you want to be with him.

My parents have an intimate relationship with God, but I think I noticed it more when they weren't so busy.

Jessica M., age 16

Families that only work together or that are so busy that they see each other only in passing become autonomous. They may share the four walls of a house, but the real walls develop in relationships as family members become isolated from one another. Is there a time that is convenient for both you and your teen? Mark that day on your calendar and set it aside just for family time. Tossing a football around the backyard with your teen means that you have carved out time just to spend with him. If you want to make it a date, ask your teen for her ideas. Be adventurous. Be willing to compromise. You might ask her to go to the theatre, but then the next event might involve an afternoon of go-carts (my favorite activity). Hiking or caving might not be cool for you, but it's great exercise. Just think "thin thighs" and understand that taking time to play together as a family might benefit you in more ways than one.

The Tie That Binds

Family is the one thing that is always there for you.

Jennifer T., age 19

How does a house become a home? It happens when the word *family* means something positive. When our teens were younger, my twins had a verbal fight at school. They piled off of the bus, offended at each other and angry. We sat them down and tried to explain that family was important, that we expected them to be loyal to each other above any other person. We wanted them to treat each other better than friends. We reinforced that over time. If family members had a disagreement, we might remind each other that, "In the Eller family, we treat each other with respect even when we disagree." Even if this went unspoken, it was still understood. It is only now that they are older and in college that we understand how powerful the bond is between our children and how much family means to each of us.

Home is not a building. Sometimes families realize this only after they lose a home to a fire or some other type of unforeseen event. It's the people inside the burning building that occupy your thoughts. Nothing else matters.

Make It Real

Our Family
Stakeholder (stāk hol-dər) ***n.***: *an individual who has a vested interest in a given situation.*

Is your teen vested in your family? Does she understand what "family" means?

These are questions that you and your teen can discuss to help gain a clear definition of what it means to be members of your family. Understanding where she fits and how the family works gives your teen a vested interest in the family.

The ______________________________ Family

1. What do we expect from each other?

2. Is there one thing that bothers you about the rules in our home?

3. What can *you* do to make it better?

4. What can *we* do to make it better?

5. Will it benefit us all?

6. What can we do together to make it better?

7. What is our purpose as a family?

8. What sets us apart from other families?

9. What are the positive aspects of our family?

Helpful Hints

Family Discussions

1. If you don't understand something, ask your teen to clarify it.

2. Share your own expectations. Being real with your child opens the door to relationship.
3. Don't take his suggestions as a personal affront.
4. Let her know you are listening. Reaffirm what she says by restating her comments, such as, "So what you are saying is that you feel that you don't have a say in our family vacations and you would like to help plan some activities that are fun for you as well." Restating shows your teen that you are listening, that you understand, and that you are taking what she says seriously. It also gives her an opportunity to clear up any misunderstandings.
5. Don't finish his sentences.
6. Don't form a rebuttal while he speaks. Wait until he is completely through sharing before responding.
7. Understand that every expectation might not be feasible. This is not a candy store wish list, but rather an opportunity to consider each opinion—getting things out in the open where real communication can begin.

Chapter Eight

Do You Have a Minute?

Your neighbor is the man who needs you.

—Elbert Hubbard

Question: Would you rather have a $200 gift certificate to the mall or a weekend with one or both of your parents?

As a normal teenager, I would choose the gift certificate. But now that I think about it, the last time I spent a whole weekend with my parents was ... NEVER, so I would like to spend the weekend with them.

Diana C., age 16

Sitting on metal bleachers watching a child play basketball or going to a school play might not seem like fun to you, but it means the world to your teen. The Greek definition of the word *time* is "honor." A secondary definition is "the value of a person." Your presence and time honors your teen and demonstrates that you value him as a person.

One teen I interviewed was raised in a dysfunctional home as a child. His biological father abused alcohol and mistreated him. He was removed from the home and later adopted. During his teen years, his adopted parents had a change of heart. He lived with friends while he finished high school. I asked, "When you become a parent, what is the one thing you will do differently?" He responded that he would do many things differently, but if he could only choose one, it would be to support his kids. He listed several different ways he wanted to put that into action. None of the ways had to do with material things. They all centered on spending time with his future children. For this eighteen year old, time definitely represented honor and value.

I would take the weekend with my parents because the memory would last forever instead of worldly possessions that would be thrown out in a month.

Kinsey P., age 16

This Is a Hard Question!

Well, if I was selfless, I would go on the trip, but I don't know which! I hope I would aspire to be selfless, because, after all, being a parent makes them selfless.

Anna A., age 15

I received hundreds of fun, introspective, and sometimes sad answers when I asked teens to decide between a gift certificate and a weekend with one or both parents. Many youths struggled as they weighed the benefits of a shopping spree versus time with Mom and Dad. One teen voted for the gift certificate and then sent an e-mail the next day, explaining that she had changed her mind.

At first I was thinking, "Oh, this is easy. The money!" But when I think about it, I choose the weekend. Money and malls will always be on this earth, but my parents won't be. Some day I will lose them, and I would wish I had taken the weekend with them instead of the cold money.

Sarah A., age 15

Some teens balked at the thought of an entire weekend alone with parents, especially if they weren't getting along. They expressed sadness but decided an entire weekend might bring more pain than pleasure.

I'd choose the gift certificate, sadly. My mom can be so depressing at times, and it would be really difficult to have an entire weekend with her.

Sarah C., age 19

Those teens whose parents' marriages were stormy expressed doubt that a weekend with their parents would work out at all. The prospect of spending time with parents that might fight or argue made the gift certificates an attractive option.

I would choose the $200 gift certificate to the mall, sadly enough. I don't really think an evening with both parents would go too smoothly.

Serina-Linn C., age 16

Several shrewd teens tried to negotiate, brainstorming

ways to get both the weekend and the mall certificate. One teen assured me that if he received the certificate he would spend part of it on his family. Another promised to give a portion to charity. Nichole finally figured out the perfect solution:

I would take the gift certificate, and then my mom and I would go out for a night on the town!

Nichole H., age 15

Teens who spent a great deal of time with family presented a mixture of responses. Some chose the gift certificate, stating that they already shared special times with their parents and getting a gift certificate on top of that was a win-win situation. Others, like Kim and Amy, were just honest.

A $200 gift certificate, because I'm fourteen. I'd rather go to the mall than hang out with my parents.

Kim M., age 14

I would pick a weekend with my mom, because my dad usually gets grumpy on vacations.

Amy A., age 12

Almost one hundred percent of teens whose parents were absent due to work or other responsibilities opted for the weekend. Time with Mom or Dad was treasured because it was rare. Those teens desired what others might take for granted.

I would probably choose my mom, because we don't always get to spend a lot of time together because of her work. She comes home late, and I usually have things to do. She's tired a lot....

Ashley B., age 14

For many of the youth, spending time with family was a natural extension of the close relationships already in place with their parents. The thought of a weekend was inviting, and several of the teens expressed excitement at the prospect of one-on-one time with one or both parents.

I would choose a weekend with my mom. She is one of my best friends, and I love her to death. I absolutely love spending time with her. She's more fun than most of my friends. We have a lot of similarities, but enough differences to keep everything interesting.

Mika W., age 17

After reading through all the surveys and weighing responses in discussion groups, I came to the conclusion that time is like a stream. If the water is running and clear, your thirst is quenched. If you need more, you know where to find it and are confident that a sufficient supply will be available. If the stream trickles, you want to find a way to store the water so that you have enough to take you through the dry season. If the stream is muddy or stagnant, you want a drink only if you can find a way to get rid of the impurities. If the stream has run dry, your thirst is overwhelming.

Quality Time: Fact or Fiction?

I think I'd honestly choose the weekend with my parents. I don't really need anything anyway, and the chances I have to spend with them are becoming rare. I would enjoy the one-on-one time, and I would try to learn as much about them in that time as I could.

Jenny M., age 19

Quality versus quantity time was a hotly debated issue when it was introduced several years ago. Busy families discovered that it was impossible to be fully vested in career, family, outside activities, and other pursuits all at the same time. Quality time seemed like a valid answer. The theory was that parents could make up for a lack of a quantity of time if their children received short, focused bursts of specialized attention—quality time.

The quality time theory was not entirely without merit. Children of every age appreciate one-on-one time with their parents. Quality time encouraged parents to put distractions aside and center their attention on loved ones. However, the concept of quality time was, and continues to be, symptomatic of a culture that is controlled by the second hands on our watches. Many families only have minutes to buzz from one place to another. All over the nation, parents struggle to focus their attention on myriad demands. This culture of busyness has produced a nation of overworked, fatigued parents. It has spawned a generation of children whose lives revolve around a tightly packed schedule. It's produced teenagers who struggle to maintain deep and real contact with others because life is one quick appointment after another.

That is a hard decision. I love to shop, but I think that having a weekend alone with my parents or with just one of them would be awesome! I think that it would help things a lot. I would probably feel better about talking to them about what's going on in my life.

Amber T., age 16

Strong family relationships are not forged in fifteen-minute appointments. They are built in spontaneous moments. Strong relationships are carved when you work through problems together. They happen when you sit at the table eating dinner and talking about your day.

Quality time is a nice theory, but teens are saying they'll trade it for quantity any day. In fact, when I probed further, hanging out with Mom or Dad with no agenda was how teens defined quality time.

I believe that the breakdown of the nuclear family and this individualistic society causes people to become more isolated and lonelier. I have to look after the house on my own, so I am by myself and have no communication. I would take a weekend with my parents. Sometimes I just wish their attentions were on me.

Travis R., age 18

In our society, many youth are given increased self-sufficiency at precisely the time they need the most adult support and guidance. Teens feel they are on their own as they negotiate the choices that come with approaching adulthood. They are at a high risk for making seriously damaging life choices and crave the support and attention of their parents. Parents can tell their teens that they care for them in fifteen-minute increments, but it's demonstrated when time with family is a priority. The theory of quality time is simply not sufficient for a generation whose main foundation of support is the home.

I would choose a weekend out with my mom for the sole fact that we really get along and like to talk. I think it would be really fun to hang out, plus my mom is worth more to me than a $200 gift certificate any day.

Adam D., age 18

FAMILY IS MY PRIORITY!

What are the most significant things in your life, and how would you rate them in order of importance? Many people list them in this order:

1) God 2) Spouse 3) Children 4) Work 5) Ministry 6) Health 7) Play

Now, take an inventory of the past month and rate your priorities by the percentage of time spent on each. Actual time spent on each reveals our true priorities. If I say that something is a high priority, but it receives minimal or inconsistent time, then it's not really a priority. It's a wish list.

My parents don't have any serious flaws, but they do work a lot. We never really did have any quality family time. I am not angry. I just feel that it explains a lot about how we treat each other. There were times when I was hurt, but I knew I couldn't be mad because they were just trying to support the family.

Jezel C., age 16

Too often parents believe that loving their family means providing material things for them. Yet the teens I speak to define love in entirely different terms. Do they like nice things? Absolutely! But many teens feel the price they pay for those things is too high. It's confusing when our teens want nice clothes and cars but complain because they want time with family as well.

When I left my job to come home and be with my family, it sounded like a good deal to my young teens—until we missed the first few paychecks. We were now on a tight budget, and when the children asked for something, we had to wait until we could afford it. Expensive athletic shoes, school clothes and supplies, money for youth camp or drama tour—all of a sudden, these were luxury items. Sometimes the kids had to pitch in and help raise the money for things such as mission trips. We simply could not do it all on one income. Not long after I had left the work force, Melissa asked me if I was sure that I had made the right decision.

To be honest, I wasn't sure in the beginning. I really missed my paychecks. I missed the pats on the back. However, there were many things I didn't miss, like the commute and wearing pantyhose! My job was demanding mentally. There were many times when I had stayed late at the office to finish a project. When I was home I often thought about my next day's workload. I loved my job, but I came home from work each night exhausted. Many times I rushed to ball games to watch my kids play, sitting on a metal bench in a suit and heels. Every Wednesday night I tossed my work clothes on a hanger and threw on jeans and a shirt to race to youth group. On other nights I walked through the door and kept on working, pushing through the rest of my evening to accomplish all the things that had to be done.

In spite of this, coming home from work and living on one income seemed like a sacrifice—until I realized that my teens needed me. Who knew? I didn't, until I slowed down enough to see that they were making every critical decision in their lives and they needed me as much as they did when they were little.

I have money, and it isn't even that important to me, but I never feel like I can connect with my stepdad and my mom at the same time. I would love it if my stepdad actually cared about who I was and what I was interested in and what I thought and who I want to become.

Becca A., age 15

Today I'm back in the work force, but now I work from home. This section is not about being a working parent versus a stay-at-home parent, but rather about balancing time. The time I invested in my career, due to the commute and pressures associated with the job, elevated my career to a priority that I wasn't prepared to continue. The reality is that I was juggling so fast to keep family and work both as top priorities that I was exhausted and at times barely there, even when physically present. Today my career as an author and speaker brings in less consistent income than my previous job, but the contentment meter as a parent, spouse, and rested human being tops any material sacrifice.

Careers are only one aspect to consider when rating priorities. Our society offers a plethora of busy traps for families. It's easy to get caught on a hamster wheel of activities, lessons, and volunteer positions. We don't have to do it all. We don't have to give our kids every material thing or every opportunity. It's permissible to slow down and enjoy the simple pleasures of just being together, even if the rest of the world is still spinning wildly by.

Ministry can also be unbalanced. This happens on a personal level when ministry is placed before spending time with God. It's easy to become so busy doing things for God that a person loses sight of why she's doing it in the first place. It's dangerous when the ministry needs of others consistently take priority over family. Many teens raised in homes where parents have overwhelming ministry duties become disenchanted with Christianity. Ministry is service and sacrifice. Ministry teaches us to give of ourselves. It has the power to teach your child how to be selfless and have a servant's heart. But if a parent ministers to the world yet leaves his children to fend for themselves, priorities need to be restructured.

Time Stealers

I wish my dad would spend more quality time with me and not worry so much about work. I wish we would have more in-depth conversations without him watching TV while I'm talking.

Michelle H., age 17

Time stealers are trivial pursuits that rob us of valuable time. Some time stealers are the Internet, computer games, television, and e-mail. We don't realize how entrenched a habit can become until we try to cut it out of our lives. It's easy to fall into a cycle of mindless entertainment and miss out on productive time with family members. Many times we don't "have enough time" for family when the real issue is that we allow time stealers to take away precious moments that we cannot reclaim. God has more for us—not a legalistic list of tasks to perform, but a new way of thinking. The hours of each day are opportunities, and each moment is a possibility. It's evident that nineteenth-century pastor Nathaniel Emmons spoke the truth when he said, "A habit is either the best of servants or the worst of masters."

Time Is Ticking

There are no promises that we will have tomorrow with our teens. At best, we have a limited amount of time with our children. In the end, it will be how we spent our time—good or bad—that will make our children's memories, as well as ours. It may not seem important now, but when they leave home for the first time—or if they leave before it's time—every memory, every special moment will suddenly be viewed in a different light.

Make It Real

A Timely Prayer

Examine me, Lord, and show me if I honor each moment of my day. If I'm in a busy trap, help me to see it clearly. If there are changes that need to be made in my family, give me the wisdom to hear your voice and the strength to obey.

Help me to honor my teen by giving of my time. Help me to support my child by being there emotionally and physically.

Help me to devote my time to things that matter. Let me slow down long enough to discern what those things are.

I pray that you will give me rest physically, emotionally, and spiritually as I put my schedule in your hands and allow you to show me the way.

Get Real—Priorities

What is your wish list of priorities?

Take an honest look at the amount of time spent on each. What are your real (actual) priorities?

What can you do as a family to adjust your schedules, lifestyle, or goals to balance your priorities?

Examine your week. Are there busy traps or time stealers that rob you or your family?

If so, eliminate or curtail one of them for thirty days and substitute a healthy, fun, or beneficial activity shared with your family or a family member.

Chapter Nine

What You Teach Me about God

Faith is like electricity. You can't see it,
but you can see the light.
—Anonymous

Question: What have your parents taught you about God?

Lately she doesn't seem to care about him [God] anymore, so I don't turn to her for teaching and guidance about God. When I ask her what's the deal, she just says she got tired of all the cliché answers to her questions. I wish she would stick to what she has taught me and be my spiritual leader.

Lara M., age 17

Most of what parents teach their teens about God will never come from a Bible, but rather will be modeled by their actions and responses to life situations. Scary thought, isn't it? Our teens are watching us for cues on how to live their faith. It's humbling to any parent to know that she shapes her children's views of God. It's a huge responsibility. It's a privilege. It's one of the responsibilities that many parents overlook.

Maybe they should listen to what they are saying and take their own advice.

Diana C., age 16

We cannot fail to grasp the significance of the role that God gave us as parents. We are trusted to nurture, love, guide, and mold our children's lives. When our job is through, our teens are released to pursue their destinies as children of God. It might be difficult for you to see God's mark upon your child's life. That can happen when he is living far from God. It can also occur simply because he is a youth.

My son delights in embarrassing me in public. He has done things such as pretending to be stuck in a revolving door while hollering for me to help him. This wasn't when he was seven years old; this was recently! He and his best friend—two handsome, popular young men—were at the airport meeting us after a trip. I was the woman laughing—and walking briskly away. I always thought it was supposed to be the parent that embarrassed the teen!

It's easy to get distracted by our teens' personalities or growing pains and forget that their names are etched on the palm of God's hand. He has a plan for their lives and has marked them with destiny. What is a parent's part in that plan? What do our lives teach our teens about God?

Amy shared her story with me. Her mother was battling cancer, and her mom's courage and faith in the face of overwhelming odds taught her powerful lessons. She showed Amy how to be strong in adversity. She taught Amy how to have joy that comes only from God. Though her mother shared her faith verbally with her daughter, it was her life and how she dealt with the obstacles of life that modeled real faith.

My mom has cancer. If she survived that would be an awesome miracle for me, but I see God's love shining through her daily.

Amy A., age 12

Paul the apostle said, "Whatever you have learned or received or heard from me, or seen in me—put it into practice" (Phil. 4:9). That's a bold statement, and some might consider it egotistical. After all, aren't we supposed to blend into the background as we point the way to Christ? Aren't we flawed human beings? Do we have any business putting ourselves on the line as an example?

They taught me how to trust God and live for him on a daily basis. They weren't fake. They showed me what it meant to have a relationship with Jesus Christ.

Erin E., age 19

Your life may be the only example your teen understands. For the teen who already knows God, your life shows her how to take the next step. Sermons mean nothing unless backed by an authentic example of faith. I have ministered to hundreds of teens who have turned away from the church and are hostile to the Christian faith because their families modeled tradition, rules, or legalism—anything other than a genuine relationship with God.

My father never talks about God, and that bothers me because I know he is a Christian. I need that from him. My mom knows a lot about the Bible, but my dad does not. Or at least he's not sharing.

Annie T., age 18

The good news is that we don't have to be perfect. We just have to be real. Our children will see us make mistakes. They will be privy to the times when we are frustrated or sad or angry, but how we respond in those times will speak volumes. Actions are the true sermons. Actions stick in our teens' hearts and minds. When we determine to set ourselves as examples before our children, we invite them to see a work in progress. We allow them to watch God minister through flawed vessels.

I think that teens need three things from their parents. First, they need to be shown so much love that it embarrasses them. Second, they need to be shown the path to walk on. They should be taught that the Bible judges this path. Third, they should know that their parents are on their faces before God praying that he will help them stay on the path. Because if they are on it, they are in God's will and everything will be all right.

Ginger L., age 19

One recent Mother's Day, an array of gifts sat on our kitchen table. I loved the fact that my children handpicked gifts that they hoped I'd love, but it was Leslie's card that made my day. When I read it, tears came to my eyes. "You have been my example," it read. "I see in you what I want in my own life." She could have given me a million dollars and it would not have meant as much to me as those words.

You see, that's all I've ever wanted. I was raised without that example, and my hopes were that my children might see God in me and be drawn to him. I wondered if that was truly possible, because there were times when I was so far from perfect. What I realize now is that a perfect parent might have only served to delay the spiritual progress in my children's lives. They saw two flawed human beings whose heart's desire was to love and serve God and one another. They heard the apologies when we messed up. They were the recipients of the tears when we confessed we had no clue what to do but would figure it out with God and with each other.

Our children hammered out their own views of God by watching their parents. That is both frightening and humbling. When we as parents realize the magnitude of our roles in our children's spiritual development, it forces us to examine what type of examples we have been—and what example we will be tomorrow.

Question: What do your parents do that pushes you away from God?

They don't take God seriously, and they let the world affect their faith. They don't always practice what they preach. I want an awesome, faith-filled example from them. An unspoken thing they taught me was that God is just going to church and meeting friends, sometimes just a social gathering. Also that salvation is good deeds.

Sarah C., age 19

Parents have the power to push their teens toward or away from God. Living by example is the first step to guiding teens to a deeper relationship with God. Examining that example is the next phase. Teens discussed with me six mistakes a parent can make when trying to teach them about God.

Mistake #1—Make Everything a Religious Issue

I wish that they would tone it down sometimes. My mom often says to pray for things such as a lost shoe. Although I know that God could help me find the shoe, this is not the help I'm looking for.

Becky S., age 18

A teen was preparing dinner with her mother. As she pulled the pot of macaroni-and-cheese off of the burner, she noticed that something was wrong. The cheese stuck to the bottom of the pan. Burnt, soft noodles swam to the top of the gooey mess.

"What in the world did you do?" her mom asked. She grabbed the recipe and read the directions out loud to her daughter.

The girl grimaced. "Milk? I thought you used water. That's what I use in the instant stuff."

The mother tossed the recipe book on the counter. "I thought you were a Christian. If you were, you would follow directions. Isn't that what the Bible says?"

Uh, no. It doesn't.

Faith is about obedience. It's not about mac-and-cheese. This teen was ripe for a lesson on how to read a recipe. That's a life skill that has nothing to do with religion. If a parent uses Scripture or faith to make everything a religious issue, it turns a teen off. In fact, it turns pretty much everybody off.

I've met adults who twist every topic, current issue, or discussion into a Christian life lesson or sermon. I love talking about the things of God, but when the gospel is used to debate, humiliate, or irritate, we teach that God is poised above like "Boomerang God." Do one thing wrong and he beams down from the clouds to hammer you and then he's gone! This is a distorted image of God that teaches our teens that God is petty and vindictive and that he's consumed with regulating every detail of our lives.

My parents share their faith by preaching to me at every little comment I say, but they've taught me nothing much about God.

Eleanor T., age 16

When we use Scriptures to shame teens into obedience, we teach teens that Christianity has to do with clothes, hairstyles, or clean bedrooms. These teens may fail to grasp the fact that obedience is a heart issue. I have heard teens make a long list of things they do right to explain the depth of their faith. They read their Bible; they don't swear; they don't drink; they don't associate with unbelievers; they don't listen to secular songs. These are all good things, but when I challenge them to take it deeper and ask them why they do these things, the answer usually has little to do with running after God's heart and everything to do with the outward trappings of appearing "Christian."

The deeper problem with this mindset is that their faith is more about them and their good deeds and less about Christ. If they don't hear from God when they think they should, they parade their lists before God and ask him why he didn't respond to them. This is self-righteousness, and it's a learned behavior. Our job is to strip away that façade and teach our teens to make daily decisions simply because they love God and want to be in his will. Our teens need to understand who God is and that it's not our works that he is after, but our lives and our love.

A parent is responsible to use the Scriptures to impact the hearts of their children, rather than using Scriptures as a battering ram. We can share the Scriptures to point them to God. We can sit with them and show them how to study the Bible and allow God to teach them how to live. When their faith becomes personal, teens change from the inside out, rather than from the outside in.

Many teens miss the message of grace and mercy. They wonder, "If God gets mad over something like not following directions to make mac-and-cheese, what will he do if I make a serious life mistake? Why even try?"

Mistake #2—Fail to Take It to the Next Level

They really only taught me the basics. They never went into depth about the Bible or anything like that. I wish they were more into religion to set a better example for me.

Samantha W., age 19

I wasn't raised in church, and in some ways that gives me an advantage over my own children. When I encountered God, he rocked my world. I didn't believe he existed, and when I discovered that he was real and that he loved me, it changed me forever.

They taught me the ABCs—how you have to go church.

Troy M., age 18

My children were on the pew the third day after they were born. We have attended the same church for over twenty-three years. They have heard 10,000 sermons. They've heard every Bible story. It's easy to take faith for granted when it's familiar.

My parents have taught me everything about God, but perhaps that's why I have trouble with God. It's all so familiar, and nothing seems new. I know that growing up in a Christian environment is not something to be taken for granted, but it blows for my faith life.

Karianne P., age 17

Parents make a mistake when they think that youth will develop an intimate relationship with God simply because they attend church. In fact, it's harder in some ways because they have to sort through what is personal and what is learned. When I came to Christ, my private relationship was formed in that moment. My children have had to build their own altars. Christianity was a part of their family life from the beginning. They had to sort out what exactly their beliefs were apart from tradition and family values. There comes a time in every "church kid's" life that he or she has to separate these and serve God on a one-on-one basis. Many teens fail to do this and discover later in life that the family altar is not enough to carry them through tough life circumstances or choices. Tradition was sufficient in the family cocoon, but it fell apart when they didn't know how to live for God on their own.

I can't remember not knowing about God. It's hard to distinguish what my parents have taught me and what my church has taught me. I guess just watching how my parents get up early and pray and read their Bible every morning has taught me a lot about faithfulness.

Beth R., age 17

Parents can take faith to the next level by talking about God in the home. Talk about what God means to you. Discuss faith in real terms and in light of real world issues. What does the Bible say about times of unrest? Who can we trust when our world is in conflict? Sometimes your teen will have difficult questions. You are not required to have all the answers, but you can see how God works in the midst of that problem or situation.

They taught me that he is awesome, that no thing or person can compare to him. He is forgiving, and that is all I need to do [ask for forgiveness] when I have sinned. He changes people for him. He sends his Spirit to help in our lives. He is love, and through his son, Jesus, we can have eternal life. There is so much more! About the Bible and so much stuff, but I can't write it all down.

Sarah A., age 15.

You can discuss Scriptures, remembering to keep them in context, or talk about how Christ modeled faith in similar situations. This might seem intimidating to some parents because your teens might have very different viewpoints, but that's part of the spiritual process. They are on a journey to carve out their own relationships with God.

My dad is a teacher of biblical studies at a college, and it's really fun to talk with him about stuff like evolution.

Kyle G., age 14

Discussions allow you an opportunity to search the Bible

together with your teen to see what God has to say on the issue. It's not an opportunity to preach (see Mistake #1), but an opportunity to talk with other believers or seekers about God. Present the information; then let your teen grasp it and apply it. Don't be afraid to talk about your faith on a deeper plane than "How was Sunday school?"

They have taught me Sunday school songs and stories, but I don't believe that we've gone deeper than that. They don't ask me what happened at youth [group], which I would really like, since some amazing things have happened to me there. I've never shared it with them because they've never asked.

Grace B., age 13

MISTAKE #3—HYPOCRISY

It would impact my faith if they lived their faith beyond reproach. No hint of hypocrisy or complacency in their lives.

Keith J., age 21

Hypocrisy destroys the budding faith of our teens. It sends a message that faith is for social purposes or is a convenient crutch. They hear this from their unbelieving friends, and it is affirmed by a hypocritical parent's example. Hypocrisy cements the belief that Christianity is not any better than the other available belief systems. A powerless life that lacks relationship with God is not only uninviting; it's repugnant—and yet parents often wonder why teens walk away from Christianity.

Real faith compels your teen to experience intimacy with God. It stirs a desire to lay down self-interests and pick up the cross. It's vital that parents understand that Christianity is not an easy choice for teens. What does your teen see in you that will help him make that choice?

The basic church thing—that he [God] is the right way. They claim they have an intimate relationship with God, but I sometimes wonder if they are telling the truth or what?

Pete D., age 18

The mask of hypocrisy is a clear message that faith doesn't really matter. Parents who live a hypocritical life create stumbling blocks for their teens' spiritual journeys. Teens are looking for someone to demonstrate the power of a living Savior. They are searching for those who live their faith with authenticity. They are so inundated by messages of "spirituality" that Christianity stands out only when it is demonstrated in the life of a committed believer.

Parents can impact their teens' faith if they live in faith every day. Practice trusting God and encourage your children to do the same.

Michelle A., age 19

Hypocrisy is pretending to be a man or woman of faith yet living a noncommitted or sinful lifestyle. It's imposing double standards. There are many ways to do this, but let's simplify it. A double standard is expecting one thing from your teen and something else for you. Both parent and child should share one biblical principle. If a movie is not acceptable for teens because it has explicit sexual scenes, then it's not suitable for parents either. The standard has nothing to do with age, but with the underlying principle. Ask yourself: Does watching this movie with explicit sexual images honor God and my relationship with him? If the answer is no, then the rule applies to both the teen and the parent.

The one thing my parents could do would be to set an example.
Troy M., age 18

Mistake #4—Fail to Support Youth Activities

I am growing by leaps and bounds in my youth group. It was only two years ago that I was painfully shy and self-conscious about everything I did. Now I can actually talk to people happily and am making friends. I am constantly being stretched to love God more passionately, to pursue Him more wholeheartedly, to live more cleanly, and to minister more to those around me than ever before.
Amanda B., age 18

A few years ago a teen stood outside the church. She had been gone for several weeks and had not responded to phone calls. It was dark, so I couldn't see her very well. I walked over to tell her hello. I was dismayed when I realized that she was pregnant. She wrapped her arms around me and gave me a hug. She didn't see it in the darkness, but a tear slipped down my cheek. I hate losing battles with our teens! We stayed for a few minutes and talked further. "So, what are you going to do?" I asked. She chatted about the baby, and it was clear she had no clue what was ahead.

Later that night as I sat in my living room my heart was heavy from our conversation. I remembered standing outside the youth door of my church after an awesome service a few months earlier. The youth pastor was just about to deliver an altar call, and several youth were visibly moved. There was a handful of teens in the youth group who were not living as believers. They came to church because they had to and sat in the back row. This girl was one of them.

She sat with her head in her hands, and I could see that the Holy Spirit was tugging at her heart. Her parents stood outside the main doors of the youth room, impatient because the service was running late. They asked if I would go get her. I glanced back through the door, knowing it would only be a few more minutes. I asked if it was possible for them to wait just a moment so I wouldn't disturb any of the teens. I hoped the girl would respond to the altar call. I prayed that the parents would wait just a few more minutes and be sensitive to what God was trying to do, but it didn't happen. The father pushed past me to retrieve the teen and her siblings.

I wonder what she lost that night. What was God waiting to do in her life? Would he have directed her life down a different path? Would she have felt God's presence? We don't know, because that opportunity was taken from her. The timing was inconvenient. The service was running later than usual, but what God was doing was so important.

I haven't learned anything about God from my parents except that he exists.

Meredith G. age 18

Do I sound frustrated? This is probably the biggest struggle I have as a youth worker, and I'm not alone. Family support is something discussed among youth workers in every church. It's critical that a teen has support in spiritual activities. Youth pastors and youth staff have a couple hours on Wednesday night and Sunday morning to teach and encourage students. We know that they will be bombarded with real life decisions all week long, and we want to work as a team with parents to impact their children.

My parents allowed me to go on a trip overseas. It changed my whole outlook on what is out there in the world.

Kim R., age 19

Every youth event, every mission trip, every drama tour, every time teens gather with other teens and adults who love God, there is a possibility that they will be strengthened in their faith. If teens are still seeking, they have the opportunity to feel the presence of God and respond. As a speaker, I've watched helplessly as parents pulled teens out of altar calls because they were ready to go home. It makes me want to take the parents on a tour of the world in which their teens live and ask them if they realize how much their teens need the presence of God. Parents will sit on cold, metal benches and cheer a basketball team until 10:00 P.M. on a weeknight. They'll wrap up in blankets when it's raining to watch their sons play football. Yet they fail to understand that their teens need support for youth-related church events as well. If you deliver your teen to a youth event or have been asked to pull out one more dollar for a youth activity, I pray that you will do it with a cheerful heart, for you are investing in your teen's spiritual life.

I always go to church, which I'm really starting to appreciate.

Janelle T., age 15

I've called youth who missed church and discovered they were grounded from a youth activity. Grounding your teen from church activities sends the message that church is just one of many activities—but it's the one he needs the most if he is making bad decisions. Ground him from the television, the phone, or his computer, but don't deny him the possibility of a life-changing experience. During fifteen years of working with teens, I've noticed it's the teens who need the most support who receive the least. When parents make an effort to help their teens become a part of church youth activities, events, camps, and mission trips, they create opportunities for their teens to connect with God and take their faith and ministries to a deeper level.

If I could tell my parents one thing, it would be to support me more with the activities that I do within the church.

Rebekah A., age 20

One ministry concept in youth evangelism is that teens must belong before they will believe. They have to have ownership in the church or youth group. By supporting your teen in youth group, youth activities, and extra events, she has ownership. She belongs.

I think what has impacted my spiritual walk the most is mission trips. I've been on two month-long trips with Teen Missions International, which really gets you out of your comfort zone for a long time. It makes you think a lot more about your walk with Christ when you get back. Sure, my youth group helps and everything, but it's my mission trips that have made me want to care. I think wanting to care about your walk helps you grow.

Stan T., age 16

What about mission trips? They are expensive. Your teen is flying away to an unknown country with unforeseen challenges. Are they really necessary? Mission trips change teens' lives. Mission trips expand their horizons by giving them a glimpse of what it means to be selfless. Trips show them a world outside of their own little clusters. Do you want to contribute to something that will open your teen's eyes to the possibility of being used by God? Help her raise the funds to go on a mission trip with your church youth group or a reputable youth organization.

My parents just recently allowed me to go on a mission trip that changed my life. My parents were willing to pay a large sum of money to let me go. When I got back, they saw I was changed. They have been wonderful by accepting the changes and talking to me about my faith and the mission and good things like that. It has been amazing. It really shows how much they care.

Sarah A., age 15

Right now, there are parents who are on their knees crying out to God for their unsaved teens. They are praying for the teens who are on drugs, who are in rebellion, or who don't want to live because life is too overwhelming. They are investing time spiritually in their teens because their children walked away from their faith. Rather than complain about the youth group or youth activities, consider how blessed we are to be able to support teens who want to be involved in spiritual activities. If your teen is running toward God, take a moment and thank God—and then run with him.

They've taught me about his goodness. They've shown me through their examples the value of faith in him and only him.

Jenny M., age 18

Mistake #5—Micromanage My Faith

My parents give me the space to develop my own personal beliefs.

Mika W., age 18

Put on that juggler's cap, because we are going to talk about balance one more time. Supporting your teen's youth activities cannot be confused with micromanaging your teen's spiritual life. The best that you can do is to show him the way, but if you try to live his faith for him it will backfire. It's great to have family devotions but another thing entirely to hover over your teen while he reads the Bible to make sure he gets in his five chapters.

God does not force us to follow him; why should parents force us to follow him? Make sure that it is the most important thing in your own life.

Keith J., age 21

Parents can discourage teens when they regulate Christianity. Teens might feel as if they are punching a spiritual time clock. In my discipleship class we adopt the concept of sevens: Live for God seven days a week and connect with him every single day for seven minutes. It doesn't sound like much, and it's certainly not enough, but it's a start. Many teens feel overwhelmed at the thought of being alone with God. What will they say? What if they don't understand the Bible? What if they can't spend an hour in prayer and Bible study? Does that mean that they failed God?

An hour may not be feasible; however, seven minutes is attainable. Anybody can read a chapter of the Bible and talk to God for seven minutes. The beauty of this concept is that it becomes less about how much time to spend in prayer and Bible study and more about connecting with God every single day. Most teens find that seven minutes turn into ten and then into thirty—and some realize they've been in their alone times for an hour or more. The concept of sevens took the pressure off the teens in our group. Now several students have vibrant prayer lives that mirror those of mature adult Christians.

Live by example. Let her see it in you first. Read the Bible and foster your own love walk with God. Have family times where you can talk with each other about spiritual matters. However, when your teen closes her bedroom door to pray or read the Bible, don't ask, "Did you pray for a half hour like you said you would?" Encourage her in her faith, but don't make the mistake of teaching her that reading the Bible and praying is about pleasing you instead of connecting with God.

MISTAKE #6—DROP ME OFF AT THE DOOR

Question: Do your parents go to church with you?
Do you want them to?

My dad is a Christian, but he doesn't go to church. That is really hard. It would help a lot if both my mother and father attended church together.

Amber L., age 17

Across the nation, thousands of teens are dropped off at the church door or arrive with friends. One-third of the 200 teens who attend my home church come alone. According to teens, it makes a difference when Mom and Dad make faith a family affair. I was a teen who attended church alone for the first two years after I was saved. It was hard to kneel at an altar and feel God's presence and not be able to share that with the people I lived with.

My mother goes with me. That's a blessing, because I have friends whose parents don't believe. That affects them.

Vickie M., age 21

There is a distinct dividing line in youth groups. There are those teens who have family support in church and those who do not. Parents who attend a church are aware of activities. They know what their teens need to be plugged in to youth group and events. They work with their teens to raise funds for trips and activities. Many of them volunteer as camp counselors or youth sponsors. They know the names of the teens in the church and know them on a personal basis. They make sure that their children attend Sunday school and small cell groups. These teens are not just tied to the youth group, but to the entire church family.

I love the people I am in community with. It helps strengthen my faith as a new Christian to see God alive in my church. My parents would impact my faith if they would come to church with me and try to understand my spiritual journey, rather than just saying, "That's nice, dear."

Travis R., age 18

Those teens whose parents do not come to church are usually less connected with the church. Many of them attend youth service only. They might not attend camp or weekend activities because their parents see them as unnecessary or too expensive, unaware of their spiritual significance. Younger teens who do not drive might not have a way to Sunday school or discipleship groups. Many of these teens feel disconnected. There are exceptions in every youth group, but typically a family that attends church together is a support system for its teens. It's a family affair!

My parents could impact my faith if they would believe it themselves!

Gemma M., age 13

When teens from non-Christian backgrounds do accept Christianity as a lifestyle, they carry their newfound faith to a home where it's neither understood nor nurtured. One girl who comes to my home church does so against the wishes of her family. It's not uncommon for teens to miss church because they have to choose between church and other activities that their parents consider more important. Many teens feel alone in their faith when family support is nonexistent. When I asked teens to tell me the one thing that parents could do to impact their faith, the overwhelming response was for their parents to go to church with them.

The one thing my parents could do to impact my faith would be to come to church with me.

Becca A., age 15

TAKE THEM ON THE JOURNEY

Question: Do your parents have an intimate relationship with God?

My parents have taught me about his goodness. They've shown me through their examples the value of faith in him.

Jenny M., age 19

You teach your child about God when you include him in

your own journey. Share with him your love and excitement for God. Show her the things in God's Word that excite or teach you. Be open with your faith and your joy in knowing God. If God touches your life in a special way, allow your teen to celebrate with you.

My family is very faith-oriented. My parents have taught me that even through cancer and losing money there is no reason to be mad at God. Those times are just to make you stronger in your faith.

Jennifer T., age 19

All families go through difficult times such as sickness, financial difficulties, or unexpected crises. What does your teen learn from you during those challenging seasons? You have a chance to show her faith in action. Talk to her about God's faithfulness and how you are trusting God. Share with him how God is teaching you and guiding you through the hard times. Let him know that God can walk with you and help you find a way through the dark times.

When I discovered that I had cancer, I discovered that I had less than a forty percent chance of surviving over a period of five years. I sat with my children and shared with them my faith that God would be with us every step of the way. I remember Melissa, then only eight, sitting beside me with her Care Bear™ blanket wrapped around her as we prayed together. She told me how frightened she was that I was sick. I told her that God cared about how she was feeling and that if she prayed he would give her peace. Later that night she brought me her children's Bible. She had opened her Bible and a Scripture of comfort was the first passage she read. She was so excited to know that God had heard her prayers.

When I went through chemotherapy and radiation, I was honest with my children. I told them that I was intimidated by what I would face without giving them scary details. I told them that I planned to trust God. After our family discussion, my daughter Leslie pointed to her feet. "Mom, God can do anything," she said. Leslie was born with severe clubfeet and had extensive surgery. She was told that she would not be able to run or play sports, but she played both soccer and basketball.

My children were my greatest encouragers. This was one of the hardest times in our lives, but we grew in our faith as a family as we faced it together. They still remember that time in a positive light. They don't remember being frightened, but they remember that time as an adventure as we watched God help us through the entire process. I am a cancer survivor of twelve years now. A lot has happened in that time. We've faced struggles, we've delighted in good times, and we've had the chance to include our teens in every step of the journey.

Everything I know about God is good, and I love them [my parents] for that. Anytime I have questions they are there with the answers.

Salena B., age 18

Let your teen know that God is real to you. Be transparent in your faith walk. Show him that God is more than tradition. He's a way of life. Include your teen in the adventure.

MAKE IT REAL

How Do I Teach My Children?

The Scriptures encourage us to examine our lives. Though you might discover some things that you wish you hadn't, celebrate! Ignorance simply means that we are unaware. Knowledge of what is wrong gives us the ability to make changes for the better. Use these questions to help you search your heart.

1. If my life were a sermon, what would it be?

2. Do I use Scripture or religion in discipline?

3. Do I evaluate my child's spiritual life according to life issues (such as thinking that making bad grades makes you a poor Christian)?

4. Do I have a different set of standards for myself than I do for my teen?

5. Do I support my teen's youth activities with a cheerful spirit or with a grudge?

6. Do I know my teen's youth pastor and support him or her with prayer?

7. Do I micromanage or regulate my teen's spiritual progress? Have I taught her that it is a duty?

8. Am I more concerned with my child's faith than my own?

9. Do I include my teen in my spiritual challenges and triumphs?

10. Do I talk about real issues in the light of faith with my teen?

11. Have I ever complained about my teen's involvement in church?

12. Do I attend church with my teen, or do I drop him off at the door?

A Prayer

Light me up, God. Let my life be an example to my teen. If I have double standards, forgive me, for I have not only sinned against my child, but against you. If I have complained about your temple, help me to see that it is where you live and breathe and move. I want to feel you, to learn about you, and to grow in my faith in the house of God.

Restore my joy in you, precious Savior, so that my teen can see what it means to know God. Help me to focus on my own faith and allow my teen to serve you with a willing heart. If I have frustrated my teen's faith, help me start fresh today.

Lord, my teen hears so many spiritual truths that sometimes it is difficult to know what is truth and what is not. Make my faith real so my teen will have a living example of what it means to be a follower of Christ. Restore my first love with you so that my teen sees you in me.

I need you as a parent, Lord, but first and foremost, I need you as a child of God.

Chapter Ten

Relevant Family Faith

One person with a belief is equal to a force of ninety-nine who only have interest.

—John Stuart Mill

Showing is important. To show these things parents should let their kids see them truthfully. Tell them about big decisions they are faced with, perhaps, and then say what God has told them about it (through prayer and the Bible). Parents should show that God is number one by keeping a regular prayer time and sticking to his Word and giving Scripture-based advice. And even when bad things happen, parents should show their unswerving faith in the Lord. Putting God first always is an awesome example.

Sarah C., age 19

We know that our lives teach our children, but where do we go from there? What do teens say they want from their parents in terms of faith? How do we involve God in our families in a way that it will transform our teens?

Question: Do your parents ever pray with you?
Do you want them to?

Let's begin with prayer. Teens do want parents to pray for them, but they aren't talking about quickie prayers over tacos or prayers cloaked in sheep's wool—you know, prayers like, "Dear God, help Suzie to figure out how to be obedient so she will stop back-talking." Quickie prayers have little impact. Sermon-prayers push your teen one step away from you and a giant step back from faith. Teens want to know that their parents are praying for them on a daily basis. They believe that a parent's prayers protect them and help them, even when they are struggling.

Praying for us really helps. Prayer softens hearts, and I am living testimony of that. Now I'm praying for my brothers.

Anna A., age 15

A nineteen-year-old teen knocked on our door in the middle of the night. His parents called me earlier to let me know that he might come by, though none of us thought that would be at 2:00 A.M. Corey stood on my doorstep. He was completely stoned but was immaculate otherwise—the perfect GQ picture, handsome and wearing the latest fashion.

Corey's outside portrait failed to show the war that raged within. He was an addict, but no one was quite sure how he had arrived at that place. He was raised in a good home. His parents were active in the church and successful in the community. His mother was at home each day and was the cookie-baking, PTA kind of mom that every child loves. His parents' marriage was strong and loving. They had two children, both of whom were great kids, and everything seemed to be on course—until Corey turned sixteen.

He took his first hit at a party and, within a few months, he was using meth on a regular basis. Corey became a master at keeping his two lives separate. Somehow he disguised his addiction from his parents, his closest friends, and his youth pastor until the night he was picked up for a DUI and his secret world came crashing down. He was sentenced to community service and fined. His parents were shocked but immediately stepped in to support him with unconditional love—and also backed the court's decision. They enrolled Corey in a substance abuse program and began to pray.

When Corey left the program, he went back to his former habits. This time he didn't hide it. He broke curfew. He came in high or not at all. His behavior at home was erratic and sometimes violent. He was running with a dangerous crowd—people who lived in the underbelly of the small city, who carried guns and used them, who cooked meth in dilapidated houses and tiny hotel rooms.

In the space of six months, this family's life turned upside down. Nothing had prepared them for the situation. Corey's addiction was not only destroying him; it was shattering his family as well. Corey's parents never knew what to expect. They set boundaries and he broke them. They struggled to find a handhold on their faith to take them through these uncharted territories. After a few more incidents, Corey was given an ultimatum. He could attend a Christian rehabilitation program and turn away from drugs and that lifestyle, or he had to leave home. He refused treatment. The poor behavior continued, and his parents asked him to leave. It was a decision that broke their hearts, but they were desperate, clawing through the agony of trying to decide what would best serve their son.

Corey had been on his own for a few months the night he arrived on my doorstep. My husband watched nearby as I stepped onto the front porch. "What's up, Corey?" I asked.

"Tell him to stop!" he shouted. He started crying. He spoke rapid fire, his sentences running together and incoherent. I desperately tried to follow the conversation. I asked Corey to sit down.

"What are you talking about?" I asked.

He put his head in his hands. "Every time I go home I hear him. He's in his room praying for me. I hear him asking God to save me. It's not fair. As long as he prays for me, I can't give up. If he would just stop praying, God would leave me alone."

I sat in the darkness with the broken young man beside me. The wide-open sky was dotted with distant stars. The omnipotent presence of God was tangible. The prayers of a father, though grieved and broken, were so strong that they were reaching into the darkest regions of his son's soul and stirring him.

The one thing my parents could do for me to impact my faith is to pray for me.

Jennifer L., age 15

The final chapter of Corey's story is not yet written, but I firmly believe that there will be a positive ending. Corey is still struggling, but he's in a Christian rehabilitation program. Every time we speak I see a desire in his eyes to find a way out of the addiction and back to his old life.

I've heard parents say that there comes a time when you just give up—and yet Corey's parents continue to believe that God can and will heal their son. They have stood firm, and their son has been cloaked in love. There is heartbreak, but determination. They understand that the decision to give his life—his addiction, his dreams, and his future—to God must be Corey's. They also know that prayer is powerful and effective. I'm not sure where Corey would be without his father's prayers.

My mom just prays and asks the Holy Spirit to talk to my heart about things since I've gotten older.

Michelle H., age 17

It's a mistake to only pray for our teens when they are struggling. A parent's prayers are a covering over his teen's life. We have no idea what God is doing with those prayers as our teens face temptation or make decisions that can be life altering. A parent's prayer is a marker in life that helps teens turn right or left as they contemplate their futures.

Praying with Your Teen

My dad used to pray with me, but it was just reciting a prayer mostly, not truly praying. If it were real prayer, that might be cool.

Sarah C., age 19

Though teens are comforted to know that their parents are praying *for* them, many are uncomfortable with the thought of praying *with* their moms or dads. Teens view prayer as a vital part of their relationships with God. Having a parent join in prayer with them is like having Mom or Dad eavesdrop on a private conversation.

Whoa, I have to say I probably wouldn't like having my parents pray with me. I don't really know why. Maybe it's because you are supposed to be honest with God because he knows stuff anyway. If you are praying with your parents, then you have to be honest with them, too. Maybe it feels like they would be invading my privacy. I'd feel really uncomfortable with that now.

Stan T., age 15

Teens can talk to God about anything. Prayer is their secret place where they can meet with God and confess their sins or ask for strength in the midst of a challenging situation. They can share their dreams for the future or rejoice in a word spoken to them through the Bible. They can pray for an unsaved friend who had sex with a guy the weekend before. They can be totally honest with God. They want it to be a personal conversation—and hope that their parents will give them the space to allow that to happen.

I don't want my parents praying with me because it would just feel weird to have them know stuff about my life.

April W., age 14

The teens in my discipleship class keep prayer journals. For some of them, praying is difficult because they are still maturing spiritually. Writing their prayer needs and thoughts in a journal is much easier. A parent caught me after service one night and told me how excited she was that her son was spending time with God. She then shared the fact that she read her son's prayer journal every day. "It's so awesome to see what he has to say," she said. Though her motivations were pure, if her son discovered that his prayer journal was open for family viewing, chances are his prayer entries would cease altogether. The reality is that he wasn't writing in his prayer journal for an audience of two.

I don't know if I would want my parents to pray with me or not. For me, praying is a very spiritual, personal thing between me and God. I think it would lose that if I were to share it with another person.

Mika W., age 17

Discern Private Versus Family Prayer

I don't want my parents to pray with me. I just don't feel right talking about my problems and asking God questions with another person.

Tim B., age 16

It's important, then, to distinguish between teens' private prayer times and family prayer. Your teen's private times with God are his own. Family prayer is about family issues. It's praying for guidance and blessing. It's a time to praise God for the big and small events that affect your family. It's praying about the world in which you live.

Family prayer should consist of real prayers rather than canned prayers or a recitation over dinner. It doesn't have to be lengthy, and it's better if it's not. Some parents like to put a time clock on prayer, scheduling it in during the day. In this overscheduled world in which our teens live, scheduling prayer can make it seem like one more duty. Rather than worrying about time, concentrate on content. Make family prayer informal and open. Allow each member to talk to God as if talking to a friend. If a family member wants to participate silently, honor that. Many teens love God but are not comfortable praying in front of others, even family. Family prayer can bring members closer as they pray for God to bless and guide their family. It can be a solid rock in times of wavering crisis. Family prayer is a time to reflect on the things for which we are grateful.

I want our family to pray together. There is a strong bond and connection within a family that prays together, and unfortunately we do not have the spiritual glue in our relationships with each other. My sisters and I pray together, but our parents do not pray with us.

Lacynda B., age 20

EXPERIENCE GOD IN THE UNEXPECTED

I recall one memory of true emotional prayer with my parents. We went to a place in Arizona with natural burnt-red canyons and mountains. There was a church up on a hill of the rocks, and we decided to drive to it. They had rows of candles in the sanctuary. My dad suggested lighting a candle for my uncle who had recently been diagnosed with melanoma. We held hands as my dad lit the candle and we prayed together. It is one of those times that I'll never forget.

Kayla T., age 15

We never know when a certain moment will touch the lives of our children. Stressing prayer in the home is important, but a family can experience God in the spontaneous moments. Three years ago we were on a family vacation. We walked around the city we were visiting and came upon a chapel. The building appeared to be over a hundred years old and was etched with disrepair. The massive oak doors were ajar, so we stepped in. The chapel was breathtaking from the rugged pews to the polished wood floor. A crucifix hung at the front of the church, and an elderly woman knelt at the foot of it. We stood huddled at the back, aware that we had slipped in on a private moment of prayer. The woman stood to her feet. Her shoulders were bent as she reached up and traced a path down the feet of Christ. A tear slipped down her cheek. It was a beautiful, reverent moment.

Leslie was quiet as we walked to the hotel. Later that night she told me that she had tangibly felt the presence of God in that small church. The woman's quiet devotion and love for Christ spoke to her in a way that words never had. It was awesome as we talked about how God had reached down in the midst of a busy vacation and brushed across my daughter's heart.

"God moments" can happen at any time and in any place. Watch for the unexpected moments. You never know when or where God might be waiting to touch the life of your teen—or you. Invite your teen to share in the spontaneous spiritual moments outside of the four walls of a church or your home.

FAMILY DEVOTIONS

Question: How do you wish your parents would share faith in your home?

We read the Bible and pray at meal times, but other than that it's not like, "Hey! Guess what God's doing in my life right now!"

Karianne P., age 17

The comments on this topic were as individual as the families represented. Many teens shared ideas of devotions that worked for their families. One family read a chapter from a contemporary Christian fiction book and discussed it, bouncing ideas off of each other and applying them to real life. Others read a daily portion from great devotional books with fun or creative ideas just for teens. Some had devotions late at night or after dinner. The most important thing for every teen was that faith was a natural part of the fabric of the family.

Almost every night my dad reads to us from a book (like Frank Peretti), and we all say a prayer together before bed.

Kinsey P., age 16

Some of the most awkward moments in our family came from trying to schedule family devotions. From time to time, our pastor encouraged the congregation to have family devotions, so later that night we would obediently sit in a circle and try it out. Ryan stretched and yawned the entire time. Leslie watched the door like it was an escape hatch. Melissa rolled her eyes. "How long is this going to take anyway?" she would ask. Definitely not the Norman Rockwell scene of devotions, right? Our teens were so busy that scheduling devotion time made it feel like a school project. It worked better for our family if we wove God naturally through our week. We talked about God openly with our teens. Richard and I prayed with them each night, spending a few special moments with each one before he or she went to sleep. Some of our best moments came in that one-on-one time.

I wish we had a Bible study time with the family when I was growing up. I had to learn the basics of prayer and the importance of Bible reading from other sources, though my parents did read the Bible and pray on their own.

Lanae P., age 19

Talk to your teen and brainstorm to discover what works for your family. If your teen expresses a desire for a scheduled family devotion time, include her in the plans. Let her choose a devotional book. Ask her if she wants it to be a discussion or simply a time to reflect on a passage. How you do devotions is not important as long as talking about God and biblical issues is a natural part of your family time.

During my early teens, my parents quit having the daily devotions that we had together for as long as I can remember. I miss their daily example.

Esther M., age 17

RELEVANT FAMILY MINISTRY

My father is a preacher (chaplain in the Air Force), and so I have learned a lot about God over the years. I've listened to his sermons for the majority of my life. They pray for me when things are rough. They give me advice that includes my heavenly Father. My mom has told me that you never know what is going on in someone else's life. That has always helped me to give someone an encouraging smile and to try to be compassionate. I believe that my parents have an intimate relationship with God.

Jen W., age 15

Ministry isn't limited to someone in a pastor's position. There are ministry opportunities for Sunday school teachers, bus drivers, women's ministry leaders, youth leaders, nursing home workers, missions participants, and others. Ministry can be the most enriching example we provide to our children, or it can tarnish their images of service. Most teens do not understand the selfless nature of ministry until it is demonstrated or they are invited to participate. They watch our examples to discover what it means to have a servant's heart. Ministry can be demanding, frustrating, enriching, and moving—all at the same time. Making ministry a family affair allows teens to participate in both the inspiring moments as well as the not-so-inspiring.

My pastor took turns taking his sons with him to visit those who were sick or in the hospital. Those boys learned that their father could comfort and encourage someone who was fighting a battle, but they also benefited from the special time spent with their dad. They talked while they traveled and had their father's devoted attention. As they grew older, they joined in praying for those who were sick. They saw God minister through those prayers, and it encouraged them to see prayer as a vital ministry tool. Both boys are studying to be in the ministry today.

This same family has worked to protect their kids from ministry mishaps. The parents insulate their children from the possible overbearing church member who is angry because the pastor didn't show up for her hangnail removal. If a conflict arises, it is handled at the church with order and compassion and not carried home to the family. The teens are allowed to be individuals and to pursue God at their own levels. All three of those children love God and have found their own places in the church, with their own faith.

I like my church; I kind of wish they would do more service projects though.

Kyle G., age 14

Teens define faith as service because it sets apart one faith from another. They respect selfless people who show faith through action. One night several of my teens' friends stayed the night. The next morning I was to meet some of my friends to cook lunch at a local shelter. It was my first time, and I was a little unsure of what to do. When I shared my plans with my teens and their friends, several of the teens were excited. They asked me to wake them up in time for them to go with me. They helped us cook, sat and visited with several of the people as they ate lunch, and cleaned up afterward. They were silly and fun and brought a whole new dimension to the project. They loved the idea of putting wings on their faith. (These are the same teens who will sell candy bars by the thousands to go on mission trips.)

This generation wants to know that they can make a difference. My daughter Melissa and her friends minister to the homeless in the metro area of a nearby city. They were not content to simply hand out clothing and food. They decided to live as the homeless do so that they could understand first-hand the spiritual and emotional needs of the homeless people. My daughter is a beautiful blond. She said the hardest part of being homeless for her was being invisible. Her hair was stuffed under a dirty cap. Her face was bare of makeup. She stood in the street and asked for money. The goal was to make enough money that day to eat. She didn't realize how much human interaction and human touch meant until people walked around her to avoid her. She was filthy and hungry, but most of all she wanted someone to let her know that they recognized her humanity. When Melissa shared what she had learned with me, I had trouble in the beginning getting past the fact that she had placed herself in danger, but all she saw was that she had a chance to serve and to make a difference.

This generation is looking for opportunities to be challenged in their faith walk. Relevant family faith occurs when we encourage our teens through our example and by providing opportunities for family ministry.

NOT A SPIRITUAL CLONE

I wish my parents would stop criticizing and judging me and accept the fact that my faith in Christ is personal to me. I don't publicize every moment between God and me so that they can keep tabs on my faith. They cannot live my life in Christ for me, and I will never live up to the expectations of what a "perfect" Christian daughter is, because I will never, ever be perfect, only forgiven by God's grace. That's all that God asks, is for me to live for him to the best of my ability and to allow him to work through me as he sees fit, not as my parents see fit.

Lacynda B., age 17

One of the most valuable gifts that you can give to your teen is to allow him to develop his faith life on his own. He will not be your spiritual clone, and if you expect him to be, the chances of his faith becoming personal is slim. He lives his faith in a very different environment than you do. Today's teens have opportunities that you might not have had when you were a teen. Their style of worship and music and their attitudes about service and faith might be entirely different than your own, but it doesn't make them less real.

Today's teens don't want their faith to resemble a faith of yesteryear. Where their fathers might have avoided the world, today's Christian teens and young adults take their faith right into the heart of it. They study their faith and its application by viewing it in light of current books, movies, music, and real-life issues. They are not afraid of the secular world. This makes some adults uncomfortable, because they've been taught the concept of living separate from sin. Youth believe in that same idea, but they apply it in a very different manner. Their belief is that you cannot impact a world if you confine yourself to the four walls of the church. Sin may be all around them, but if they carry Christ and the message of the gospel into the midst of it, lives will be changed.

My parents would probably want to try and change my sense of style. They don't like it. It seems to embarrass them at times.

Adam D., age 18

Teens are not hung up on the same things as adults.

They don't define Christianity by outward appearances. Just ten years ago, youth coveted name-brand clothing and looked alike with their identical shirts and expensive shoes. Today's teens might wear a cool old bowling shirt found at the thrift store. They don't care if anybody else thinks it's cool as long as they like it. They have their favorite stores, but they are an eclectic bunch. In any school or youth group, you will find a mixture from the latest styles to fun and funky clothes to sheer comfort. They experiment with hairstyles and color. They don't conform in their fashions, and they don't conform in their faith.

Since I live in a different world than you did, I'm going to do things you never got to do (like go to youth convention, be a missionary in Mexico for a week, and witness in chat rooms on the Internet). Don't try to hold me back from these things because you never got to do them when you were young. Just because you didn't do them doesn't make them wrong. And guys, I am a Christian. You often say a "real Christian" wouldn't act/talk like I do, but no one is perfect but God. You guys do and say things you know that Christians shouldn't. I love Jesus with all my heart. I know we don't talk very much about our spiritual lives around our house, but if you really knew me—how I worship, pray, read the Bible, intercede, and get all my strength from Jesus—you couldn't say I wasn't saved. Please show me a little respect.

Chad V., age 16

When we try to pigeonhole our teens into our images of Christianity, they push against us because it's not a good fit. They want to hear what God has to say on the subject and imprint it on their lives and in their world. What they have heard in the past may be very different from what they see in the Bible. Teens are studying the example of Christ and discovering that he was a maverick in his day. He didn't conform either. In fact, teens become confused when they realize that the modern church resembles the Pharisees more than a Savior who trampled on the religious folks' idea of faith.

We are all entitled to make our own decisions regarding our faith. No one forces us, but we all have decided to follow Jesus and devote our lives to God.

Kinsey P., age 16

That's why this generation has the potential to mark a world for Christ. Today's teens are taking the message to the people around them. They're asking that faith be relevant. They are fearless when it comes to throwing out traditions that have nothing to do with God or his Word. They are transparent and make mistakes. Teens are unafraid to leap out and try faith on for size in their world. They are asking hard questions about their faith and sharing the answers with their friends. I might have a chance to talk about God with an adult, but when I'm around teens who love God, I can assure you we are going to talk about spiritual matters. They don't want to settle for mere Christianity.

Believe in me. I know that it seems like my generation is always getting into trouble, but there are good kids out there. You raised me, and I think that I deserve enough respect for you to understand that you raised me right and I will make good choices. I know some of them [choices] are wrong, but they help me learn. And I know that you want to protect me, but I need to figure out some things on my own, including where I stand with God and making God my own instead of my parents' God.

Janelle T., age 15

NO MASKS ALLOWED

I believe that Christianity is seen negatively because we don't have enough people on fire for God to even begin to heal the wounds that many hypocrites in the church have caused.

Ginger L., age 19

Today's teens walk a line we never faced. They can't fake their faith because hypocrisy is challenged. The lukewarm Christian can't just blend in as he or she did when we were young. Many times the committed Christian teen feels alienated, as if he is responsible to compensate for the mistakes of past generations. Christian teens are tested to see if they will live and defend their faith and the Bible. They are asked tough questions: Why is their faith better than another? What gives them the right to say that something such as homosexuality is a sin? Who made them the judge? Because Christianity is viewed in a less than positive light, unbelievers hold today's Christian teens accountable. Our society is increasingly hostile to all things Christian. Unfortunately, we've earned some of that.

I think a lot of non-believers see Christianity in a very negative light. Many of them get preached at too much and loved too little to be impacted very much by Christianity.

Amanda B., age 18

Because of this, your teen will most likely refuse to wear masks. She will be real with you. She won't hide her mistakes or gloss over her imperfections. Sometimes this is disconcerting for adults and we perceive it as rebellion or disrespect. Actually, it's neither. Your teen has to be honest in every aspect of his faith if he expects to take it into real life. He may not conform to your idea of the perfect Christian, but he isn't trying to please man. He simply wants to follow God. Teens are ordinary people with extraordinary faith.

THE DANGER OF CONFORMITY

Don't try to force your beliefs on me. Let me make my own decisions. It pushes me away from God when you force me toward him.

Tracy J., age 15

When adults attempt to lock their teens into their versions of Christianity, it's not much different than putting a set of handcuffs on them and dragging them to the cross. It's not how Christ drew us to himself, and yet we expect our teens to follow willingly when we enforce our idealisms or timelines upon them. Teens feel like failures if they are expected to be something they are not.

When I was younger we were very open, but as I grew older I began to form my own faith in God, values and morals, and views on life. They refused to be open-minded to what I had to say, so I just stopped filling them in on what I thought or felt or anticipated in my future. I only tell them what they absolutely need to know.

Lacynda B., age 20

Jonathan was saved when he was a junior in high school. His youth group went through a period when the subject of sin was pounded into them at every sermon. They were asked to examine their lives and to give up anything that wouldn't honor God. The pastor's intentions were honorable. He was tired of seeing his kids falling into sin and seeing the results of those mistakes. As time went on, the youth group went through closets, cars, and personal items and threw away anything that might not honor God. Jonathan tried harder to fit this image, but his faith life spiraled downward as he stopped focusing on God and started trying to live by rules. Every day he tried to do better, but he felt like a failure. He was moving farther away from God rather than closer.

One day he made a huge mistake, and several people knew about it. He decided that because of this mistake there was no way that he could be a Christian. He walked away from his youth group, and he walked away from his faith. For the next five years he lived the other extreme. He drank; he experimented with drugs; he had sex and partied. He was miserable. He lived in limbo as he lived without faith but longed for God. There were times when he tried to pray, but the image of his failure and sin was too great in his mind. He decided that God could not and would not forgive him. Then, late one night as he sat in his living room, Jonathan closed his eyes and asked God to help him.

When we received Jonathan's phone call that night, I held my breath. He was my children's friend, and we loved him like he was a member of our own family. We had tried to reach out to him, but he was always politely distant. The broken voice on the other end of the line sounded desperate. He missed God so much, but he didn't know if it was possible to live for God. I reminded him that God was merciful and that he had been waiting for Jonathan to return to him.

This last year has been for Jonathan a time of shedding his old concept of Christianity and searching out what it truly means to follow Christ. Jonathan has discovered that God does forgive. He's learned that God is capable of refining a person's life when he searches for him every day. He has discovered the beauty of grace and what it means to obey God out of love rather than fear. Jonathan has inspired us as we've watched him bring several people to church with him, patiently allowing them to find God at their own pace.

I am a totally different person, but I have some of the same values that they instilled in me.

Sarah H., age 15

It's one thing to teach our teens about faith and the Bible, but another to force them to conform to our interpretations of Christianity. I'm not talking about the foundational concepts of accepting and following Christ but about the cultural and traditional rules added on over the years. This happens when adults get hung up on something like the tempo of a song (such as Christian alternative music versus the "good ol' gospel trio") and turn it into a faith issue. Adults decide that the teens can't possibly be Christians singing that loud rock music! They fail to notice that those young men and women in the bands are totally sold out to God and winning people for him by the thousands. When we label people by what they look like ("That guy can't be a Christian since he has an earring, long hair, funky clothes"—you get the picture), we act like the Pharisees, forgetting that Christ looks on the heart and not upon our outward appearances.

I wish they would share their faith by sitting down and explaining the Bible to me, along with the things I don't understand.

Sam B., age 20

How can parents teach teens about the foundation of Christian beliefs and God? Dig into God's Word together. Your teen has to be accountable in an unbelieving world, so discuss contemporary issues in the light of faith. This is an intelligent generation. Most of them expect to attain a higher education when they leave high school. They are not content to settle for less in their secular educations, and they don't want to skim the surface when it comes to the Bible either. If your youth group offers discipleship classes, support the teens as they attend. Buy books written for teens about relevant issues. Invest in Christian youth magazines that will appeal to your teen. Teach her to discern what is right and wrong by what is written in the Bible and by the leading of the Holy Spirit—but forget conformity to anything but God's Word.

Let Them Build Their Own Altars

My parents have a hard time with me saying that I have learned to place my life totally and completely in the hands of the Lord and that I will go wherever he leads me. In their eyes, I should add my own personal goals and ambitions into the picture. But I see it as an adventure with Jesus as the trailblazer and the guide. I know that my father has a very close and personal trust and faith in Christ because his life manifests his faith. However, my mother often scolds me for reminding her that God is in control when our family encounters very tough obstacles. I know that she trusts the Lord, but because

I am her child, she feels somewhat embarrassed, I suppose, by me reminding her that faith in God can move mountains.

Lacynda G., age 20

Have you allowed your teen to build her own altar? Do you encourage your teen to experience God on a personal level? Or is faith a checklist of rules of conformity in your family? Does your teen feel that if he doesn't check all the boxes, he'll get grounded, he is a loser, or he couldn't possibly measure up? Would a checklist of rules make you want to run after a living God, or would it make the running harder?

I think parents should make their children go to church, but I think that they should allow their children to begin to know God on a more intimate level in each child's individual way. Nothing is more precious than when the Lord reveals himself to someone and his or her childhood relationship with the Lord begins to turn into falling in love with him. No parent can teach that to his or her child, nor can they force discipleship on their child to make it occur. It is a heart matter.

Melissa E., age 19

There's simply a better way. Take your hands off of your teen's relationship with God and remember what it was like when you first fell in love with the Savior. Devote that same energy to your own relationship with God. Spend time with him in prayer. Read the Word—not to get a star for doing something right, but simply to connect with God every single day. Let your relationship be so real that your teen understands that you are a person who knows God on a personal basis.

Be an example for your teen. Provide a family environment of authentic faith. Talk about God, but let your teen find him in such a way that she will never want to let go.

The one thing that my parents could do to impact my faith is to let me have more freedom concerning Christianity so I can live my own faith.

Eleanor T., age 16

CHOOSING A FAMILY CHURCH

Question: Are you growing or changing spiritually as a direct result of your youth group or church?

I know that my relationship with God is primarily my responsibility, but church helps so much. I'm having great difficulty with this right now, because the church I usually attend has stopped working for me.

Meredith G., age 17

Choosing a church as a family is critical. Most adults are well established in their faith and don't realize that what works for them might not be working for their children. Is your teen growing spiritually as a result of attending your church? While the major portion of mentoring teens is on the parents' shoulders, part of that job is finding a church that offers growth opportunities for your teen. Is there a discipleship program for teens, or do they cram every person from twelve to twenty-three into one class on Sunday morning? Is there a youth program that devotes time, money, and talent to teens? Does the church understand youth culture? Do the people who invest in your teen spiritually have a passion for teens, or are they simply filling a need?

It's a sad fact, but many churches put youth as a low priority. If you love your church but it offers very little for your teen, then you might reconsider your options. Is there a church youth group across town that's rocking for Christ? If so, would you consider the fact that your teen might find exactly what he needs to make it spiritually somewhere else? Imagine the opportunities if your teen hangs out with people who are excited about God, if she can worship with a band that reaches a place in her soul that "Rock of Ages" doesn't or participate in activities that are both clean and fun!

I think that you should like the church you attend, and that's why it is so hard for me. Everyone in my church is a lot older than me. There are no other teens that attend regularly. It's a very small church, and I hate it! I don't like going, and it's a drag every week. It's so important that you get into a good church or you won't be able to grow spiritually. Everyone that can should be in a church where they have a good youth group and good friends their age.

April W., age 14

Question: How important is it for you to love the church you attend?

This is a complex but simple question. For me, it is very important to love the church that I attend. If I don't, then I will be less likely to come. I know that it is supposed to be about God, but really, I'd be sitting there thinking how much I hated the place. I am growing spiritually as a result of my youth group. My youth pastor keeps it real. The other teens are very accepting of odd styles. They don't judge me based on my appearance. I've noticed that they give a person a chance, which makes me feel welcome. The one thing they did was to actually try and get to know the real me. They took time out of their day to make sure I was okay. They didn't put on a big front that said, "Look at me, I'm churchy so I have an obligation to care." The people in my youth group are real! They mean what they say.

Pete D., age 18

It's important that your teen loves the church he attends, for an excellent youth and discipleship program can make your teen's spiritual life blossom. Many times a less than adequate youth program is exactly why teens falter. We assume they should get everything they need on their own, but that makes it so much more difficult than it should be.

If teens don't love their churches, they grow to resent them. If your teen is unhappy with your church because she isn't living for God, that's a different issue. Yet even in that instance, if there is a strong youth program in place, there are people your teen can turn to when she is ready.

Liking your church is very important because if you don't love it, how will you learn?

Alicia V., age 15

What makes a strong youth program? Leadership and churches that support the youth program, as well as dedicated youth staff members and full-time youth pastors. One of the most important factors in youth ministry is consistency. Trust is a huge issue with teens. They won't let down their guards until they know that you can be trusted. When their youth programs consist of volunteers who are rotated in and out, there is no constancy. If there is a youth pastor and other staff members who show up at every service organized, excited, committed, and invested, the teens become stakeholders in the youth program.

What about smaller churches that cannot afford a full-time youth pastor? As someone who has volunteered for almost two decades, I know that there are passionate, capable people who love youth and who will volunteer to serve. Examine the program. Are your teens growing? Do the volunteers treat the youth program like a full-time ministry? Ask your teen if the program is working for him.

Another factor is youth services. Do the youth services look like, feel like, and sound like teens? Are teen services boring, or clones of Sunday morning services? Do the services display an understanding of youth culture and music? Are they fun, loud, and exciting, as well as spiritual? Do they draw in teens and keep them coming back?

What about extra activities? Are there discipleship classes (or Sunday schools)? Do the teens fellowship? Do they have weekend retreats or attend youth camps? Friends are a critical part of your teen's spiritual development. Teens don't feel like the lone ranger when they can connect with people who love God and who will support them in their faith.

I like the church I attend very much. I go to a different church for a youth group, and at times I think I would grow more there. Finding a perfect church is not easy.

Teddi H., age 13

Make It Real

My Teen's Faith

1. Have I allowed my teen to develop her own faith?

2. Do I expect my teen to mimic my belief system?

3. Do I label things I don't understand as wrong?

4. Have I listened to the lyrics of my teen's worship or Christian music so that I could better understand why he loves it?

5. Do I expect perfection from my teen rather than a growing relationship with God?

6. Do I pray for my teen on a daily basis?

7. Does my teen want family devotions? Have I asked for her input on the material we use?

8. If my teen is open to me praying with him, what are his needs?

9. Does my teen love the church youth program? Is she

growing as a result? Is my teen plugged into a youth church that she loves, and is she with people that are a positive influence?

10. Do I respect my teen's faith and her efforts to know God? Do I tell her that?

11. Do I concentrate on my faith walk with God so that my teen will see God in me?

Chapter Eleven

Restoring Broken Relationships

Take the first step in faith. You don't have to see the whole staircase, just take the first step.
—Martin Luther King Jr. (1929–68)

I would be willing to start over for sure. Everyone needs parents. Mandy H., age 18

Do you feel as if your relationship with your teen is shattered beyond repair? Are you discouraged? Let me remind you that we serve a God who holds the universe in his hands, and yet as big as that seems, he has compassion for every person. He cares about what is happening in your home. Restoration is possible, because restoring brokenness is God's specialty.

Your damaged relationship with your teen may be a

result of mistakes that you made in the past. It may be that your teen has caused such chaos in your house that you are about to give up. You might be clueless as to how the broken relationship occurred or how to make things right again. No matter what the situation, there is hope. Even if your teen is currently rebelling or has pushed you out of his life, there are steps to take to heal that relationship.

The first step is to be focused on the relationship rather than on a list of complaints. The complaints are only symptomatic of the larger problem, which is a severed or damaged relationship. Many times parents point fingers or resort to name calling ("You're selfish and mean"), blaming ("You're destroying our family"), fighting or bickering, isolation (living as strangers in the same house), or, worse, parents give up. All of these methods drive a wedge between you and your teen. Nothing is resolved, and your relationship takes a back seat to your immediate feelings and response. You lash out or withdraw, and your teen responds in the same manner. The fractured relationship disintegrates further.

It's like since we're a family we know what things will make the other person mad, so in fighting, we try and nail our opponent where it hurts, which is wrong.

Beth R., age 17

There are two ways to deal with difficulties. We can alter the difficulty or we can alter ourselves to meet the difficulty. We might not have any idea about how to change the circumstances. We don't have the power to change what happened yesterday. However, we can affect tomorrow when we adjust our attitudes and our methods. How a parent approaches the healing process can mend the relationship or dissolve it completely.

WHEN YOU ARE RESPONSIBLE FOR THE PAIN

Question: If your parents made mistakes that hurt you (divorce, abuse, addictions), what can they do if they want to start fresh? Would you be willing to start over in your relationship?

First, [I would need to] see a complete transformation. No sign or hint of what they did anymore. Second, a heartfelt, face-to-face apology with no excuses, admitting that they were wrong and asking for forgiveness. Then, try to rebuild. Know that the kid will still feel hurt for a while and bear with him.

Michelle H., age 17

Standing at my biological father's graveside, I felt nothing. It was sad that a man had died, but I could not invoke false remorse over the loss of a relationship that never existed. They played the old Frank Sinatra song "I Did It My Way" at his memorial service. It seemed a fitting statement. He had seven children from three different marriages. The three he raised received the best and worst of being his kids. The remaining four were strangers to him and to each other. In the past forty years, I had spoken with him on three separate occasions—all at my initiation. As I stood at his graveside I thought about my own children. I couldn't imagine not knowing them. They are such an integral part of my life that I would be empty without them.

My real mom chose to live a dark and drug-filled life instead of keeping me in her life.

Jenell E., age 16

Throughout the graveside service, I looked for my father's youngest daughters—girls who were my own children's ages—but finally realized they had not come to the funeral. He was just as much a stranger to them as he was me. When I left that day, I wondered if he ever regretted that string of broken relationships.

It's just easier to stay this way than to change now, because I only have two more years of high school and then I'm out of here. I could write for hours on this subject, about the stuff my parents have done that's hurt me, but I'll spare you.

Mercy D., age 15

At the time of my father's death, I was a columnist for a city newspaper. I shared my feelings with my readers, contrasting my biological father and my real father. My real father doesn't look like me. He is short with blue eyes; I'm tall with hazel eyes. From the moment that he walked down the aisle to marry my mother, he became Dad to the two little girls who came with the package. His role of father had nothing to do with my conception; it had to do with being there from day to day, with discipline and love, with checking out the brakes and kicking the tires when I shopped for my first vehicle. His role of father was walking me down the aisle, being there for the births of my children, crying with me when I found out I had cancer, and the phone calls I still receive today, always ending with, "I love you, babes."

Absentee fathers responded to that column in droves.

They shared their stories, assuring me that my biological father must have had regrets, because they had them. Many said that the story of me standing at my father's graveside prompted them to call their own children before it was too late.

There are many parents who live with regrets because their circumstances imprinted the hearts and minds of their children. Broken homes, messed-up adult relationships, addictions, abuse, and selfish choices all shape the children who are forced to participate in the drama. They are too young to leave and too defenseless to make things better, or they are abandoned and wonder what they did to make their parent leave them.

My dad used to have a terrible temper. He was abusive more often than not. I remember when I was very little, maybe three or four, and my dad started yelling at my mom. He started throwing cans everywhere. My brother and sister were hiding behind the TV, and I was sitting at the table and started crying. My dad got in my face and started screaming that I shouldn't cry, that I was supposed to be tough and I was being a baby. He told me that I was a big disappointment. After he said this, I stood up and stopped crying and went to the living room and sat on a chair. I watched him lose his temper and watched my older sister and brother cry. I have always refused to cry after that. When I do, I beat myself up for it and punish myself somehow. I now have an issue about being too tough. My dad learned to control his temper because my mom left him until he did. She didn't take me or my brother or sister with her. She left us with him.

Lisa T., age 15

Reestablishing a relationship takes time and consistent behavior, as you are erasing memories and replacing them with new ones. When a parent does turn his or her life around, it's a wonderful day, but it's also only the beginning of the rebuilding process. Rebuilding your relationship is not a complicated process, but it's not easy either. Your teen might not trust you in the beginning. When the people that are intended to nurture you harm you instead, you form a hard shell around your emotions. It's a defensive mechanism. You choose not to be vulnerable, because letting down your guard produces pain. Many times when you see a hostile, angry teenager, you're not viewing the real heart of that teen. It's a mask. It's a clear signal that he is hurting deep inside.

I would hope that they would clean up their act and respect themselves and each other before attempting to put our relationship back together.

Kayla T., age 15

Your teen might question your motivation. Though she is glad to see that you have changed, she's still marked by the scars of the past actions or behaviors, and those take time to mend. She may test you, pushing to see how you will react, looking for the old patterns to emerge. However, your focus must be on the rebuilding process. As you grow stronger, your teen will respond to the definite changes she sees in you.

If you made mistakes in the past that hurt your family, there are four things that teens hope will happen as your relationship is restored.

#1—Tangible Changes

My parents would impact my faith just by living the life. I wouldn't know that they were Christians if I saw them from the outside.

Steven S., age 16

My mom was fragile when we were growing up. Life was chaotic and very hard at times. Yet when I look at my mother today, I see strength. I know without a doubt that this beautiful woman loves me. She shows it in a hundred different ways. She expresses her love in notes and e-mails. I have things around that remind me of her, like a burgundy crocheted blanket made with hands that ache from arthritis. The blanket is a treasured gift, but the greatest gift my mother gave me is a life that is no longer broken. Her life was transformed through her relationship with God. In the beginning I wasn't sure if the changes were genuine, but over time I forgot how things once were. The changes in her were so tangible that it altered my perception of the woman I once knew.

My home was my safe haven until I was about fourteen years old, when my mother began to experience the first symptoms of menopause and took out her frustrations and spontaneous emotions on her family and her marriage. I begged to spend nights with my friends to escape the screaming and verbal abuse. But God has done a great work in my family, and when I was nineteen, my home slowly became a safe haven once again. I believe a home is not a place or a location, but a family, a group of people bonded in love.

Lacynda B., age 20

Lip service means nothing to teens. It only hardens their resolve to distrust those who use the words "I love you," and

"I'm sorry; I did it again," in the same breath. Winning the heart of your teen won't come from giving gifts to assuage your guilt or from empty words. Winning your teen's heart will transpire as he sees you take positive steps to rebuild your life.

If my parent or parents did something to harm me, I believe that I would be willing to start over on that relationship. It would require steps on their part though. They would need to be very repentant, without casting any blame. They would have to be repentant and set the example of how to start restoring our relationship, because they are still my leaders. I would need to know that they cared about my safety. In other words, depending on how I was hurt, they would have to absolutely avoid any situation in which a possible situation could occur. This not only shows their concern not to hurt me, but also makes the abused or hurt person feel more comfortable and less awkward. Whether kids admit it or not, I've never met a hurt teen who didn't want to see their relationship restored with their parents. Their words didn't show it, but later actions did. From what I've seen in the past with friends, it takes a lot of work and attention on the parent's side. It may not be fair, but I do know it is much easier for the parent to truly lead by example in this way than for the teen.

Keith J., age 21

Examine closely where you made your mistakes and take the necessary steps to stay away from anything that might lead you back down that path. If you were an alcoholic, it may not seem like a big deal to you to be around drinking. You might believe that you are strong enough to withstand the temptation, or that taking one drink will not spiral you downward. But for your teen, one drink or being in an atmosphere where alcohol is served freely causes her anxiety because the image of you and alcohol represents pain. It is a tangible reminder of the past and she wonders if you will fail. Do what is necessary to help your child feel confident and stable by making a definite U-turn and staying away from the things that hurt you and your family. Transformation is a process, but when your teen sees you turning to God for help and making positive changes, you will encourage him in his own healing journey. He will learn to trust again as you grow together.

My mom used to go to alcohol when she felt bad, and bad things would come of that. But when she came to Christ, she went to him instead, and I saw a great witnessing tool there. She completely changed the way that she dealt with things by always going to God, even in her deepest hour, and that taught me a lot because I saw the changes in her.

Vicki M., age 21

#2—Be Honest

A new start? Well, it takes me a while to forgive and forget, so I don't know what they really could do. Probably just show me that they truly are sorry and then show me it in their life.

Stan T., age 15

Being honest about your past mistakes does not mean that you wear them like a scarlet letter on your chest. It means that you acknowledge what happened without excuses or justification. When you assume responsibility, your teen will respect you for it. Being open about the past allows you to talk about the problem from your teen's perspective. These conversations may be painful or awkward, but the issue is not allowed to fester under the surface. When it is discussed, it dies a natural death and does not hang over your family like a shadow.

When you are honest about your mistakes, your teen will have a different perspective on the events. She can only see your mistakes as she relates to them, but don't take it personally. It's not about you anymore. You're discussing someone who has been rebirthed. It's like going to a doctor when you've been given a brand new heart. The old, diseased heart no longer exists, but you talk about what caused the disease and make plans so that your new heart stays healthy and whole. Being honest about the past is good medicine, and it moves you forward to the next step.

#3—Ask, Accept, and Offer Forgiveness

I would probably just talk about what happened and pray together. I think that I might be disappointed, but I would forgive them.

Derek H., age 16

Ask for Forgiveness

If my parents did something to harm our relationship, I would like to say that I would be willing to start over, and I would try my hardest. It can be hard to forget the past. I think that would be my biggest problem. They could help me and show me that they would never let anything like that happen again. They would have to regain my trust.

Amber T., age 16

True repentance is attitude coupled with action. There is no doubt that God has forgiven you, but have you taken the time to ask your teen for her forgiveness? You might hesitate because you feel she is not ready to forgive, but asking for forgiveness has nothing to do with her response. It's an attitude of your heart. It's letting your teen know that you regret doing anything to harm your relationship. Even if she chooses not to trust you at this point, you've demonstrated a heartbeat that says, "When you're ready, I'm here." You have taken the lead, and, through your example, you are showing her how to reestablish your relationship.

Accept Forgiveness

Sometimes it's easier to ask for forgiveness from others than to receive it. One young woman shared her story. "There were times when my mom swung from out-of-control rages to depression and even threats of suicide. Living in my home was unstable at best and frightening at other times." The girl spent hours at the altar weeping over her home life and her mother, worried that one day her mother would make the threats of suicide real. One day her mother accompanied her to church to watch the girl perform in a drama and there she accepted Christ as her Savior.

Over the next several months, the mother changed her life completely but struggled with forgiveness. "I hated being stuck with all the old memories," her daughter said. "When my mother brings them up over and over, apologizing for what she did, it is a reminder. I want to move forward and start the next phase of our relationship, but that hasn't happened yet."

Accepting forgiveness means putting the past behind you. Don't confuse being honest about your mistakes with carrying guilt around like a Siamese twin. You are a new person with a fresh slate. God has forgiven you, and it's time to accept that forgiveness so that you can become the person and parent God always intended you to be.

Offer Forgiveness

The mistakes that you made might not have been entirely your fault. We can hang on to our hurts, or we can model forgiveness. My past has shaped me. It helped me to be compassionate to teens who are hurting. It inspired me to reach out and believe in teens. However, there comes a time when you leave the grisly details behind and see yourself as you are now. You press forward, leaving behind those things that weigh you down.

When we choose to forgive others, we release those painful memories. They no longer have the power to dig bitter roots in our lives. The past no longer has the ability to control your actions or emotions. Forgiving those who hurt you helps you to stop the cycle. When you forgive, you don't hand down a legacy of bitterness to your children.

Forgiveness does not mean that you invite those who harmed you or your teen back into your lives if they have not changed. As parents, your first responsibility is to protect your children. You can model forgiveness by letting go of the anger. If and when those who harmed you do change, then you have already forgiven them and will have an opportunity to extend a small part of what you've been given: unmerited grace.

#4—Don't Expect Overnight Results

Yes, I would be willing to start over in our relationship. I would want them to prove that they still care and won't hurt me again.

Linda S., age 14

The changes in your relationship will be gradual. Some changes will come in spurts, while others will come over time. You are not the only one healing. Your teen is also under repair. He is relearning how to trust. He will be wary in the beginning. Take baby steps and allow the restoration process to develop naturally.

It always depends on what they've done to break the relationship in the first place. In my case, I would love nothing else more than for my father to come to me one day, sit me down, and just apologize to my face for what he's done. Instead of trying to make up for it by protecting me and just loving me way too much. If he just sat me down one day and said, "Look, I know what I did was wrong, and I know that I can never make it up to you. I screwed up, but I would like you to know that I would like to start over, and even if I can't ever make it up, I'll try." We'd hug and kiss and even though the memories would not go away, it would be sort of a closure for the past.

Lisa T., age 15

Don't push it or overcompensate. Let the relationship heal in layers. Once your teen discovers that your progress is genuine, the protective shell will be stripped away a little bit at a time until there is nothing standing between you.

WHEN YOU ARE UNSURE OF WHO'S AT FAULT

Oh, yes, my mother and I don't get along sometimes, and I have no idea why! I think it's because our personalities clash.

Sarah A., age 15

Leslie and I were in battle, though neither one of us were willing participants. I mentally counted the reasons that she should be grateful that I was her mom. She could have made a checklist of why I should be happy to have her as my daughter. The odd thing is that we both loved each other and wanted things to be better. We had always been close, but she had retreated into silence. I heard her laughing with her sister behind their closed bedroom door, and I mourned the loss of our once-close relationship. Some would have thought I was foolish for thinking that anything was wrong. She was succeeding in her classes. She loved God. She was doing great at school and in every other area. However, there was underlying tension in our home, and it grieved me.

I know they still love me. I would always be willing to start over and give it a try.

Samuel B., age 20

Though I had worked with teens for years, I couldn't figure out how to connect with my own daughter. Other teens surrounded me on Wednesday nights, smiling as I walked in the door, running up to me and throwing their arms around my neck. It was a privilege to share my faith with them, to encourage them, and to learn from them. Parents and teens commented on how "lucky" my kids were to have Richard and me in their lives. Yet I knew that Leslie wasn't feeling lucky at all, and that's what made me sad. I had no clue how to fix it.

One day I confided to our youth pastor that I needed help. I asked if he had any books or videos that I could borrow. I was open to anything—except for his next suggestion. He asked if I would meet with other parents of teens on a weekly basis to facilitate a small cell group. This seemed like a less-than-brilliant solution, especially in light of the fact that I felt like a failure. But I was desperate, so I took him up on his offer.

Every week, a group of adults stumbled into the small room. Our children ranged in age from preteens to young adults. Parents enrolled in the class for varying reasons. Some feared the approaching teen years. Others battled problems that varied from a lack of communication to serious issues of addiction or outright rebellion. The common ground for all of these parents was a desire to connect with their teens.

It didn't take long to realize that I had a unique advantage. I knew the teens on a personal level. They had confided their needs, hopes, and desires to me as a youth staff member and discipleship leader. As the parents talked about the problems or issues that they faced, I could mentally put together the whole picture because I had heard both sides. When the two halves of a story are pieced together, the picture looks somewhat different from the one painted only by the parent.

If I could tell my dad one thing, it would be that he treats me unfair sometimes. A lot of the time he favors my brother over me. My brother is more like him, so he would rather be with my brother than with me, even though he tries not to show it. I want him to treat me and my brother equally.

Derek H., age 16

It is possible that each person has a distorted image of the problem. Perceptions are based on emotions and our perspectives as adults, parents, or teens. It is easier to find a solution when the pieces are put together.

One parent in the class was frustrated because she felt that her teen wasn't doing enough chores. The teen was taking advanced placement courses in high school to assist her in attaining scholarships for college. Her intentions were to save money because their family had a modest income. She was overwhelmed with homework. If she didn't do well in her classes, her efforts would backfire. The pressure to clean the house, complete three hours of homework, work a part-time job to pay for her car insurance, and attend church was causing her stress. When the mom heard her daughter's side of the story, they were able to come to an agreement because they both understood the bigger picture. If the daughter was playing video games and sleeping every Saturday until 2:00 P.M., then it would have been a different scenario with different results.

One day it hit me. I had been just as blind with my own daughter. I was so intent on trying to fix her that I hadn't been listening at all. I was ashamed as I remembered the times she had said, "You're not even hearing what I'm saying, Mom." The picture might look entirely different if I allowed Leslie to clue me in. By focusing on the real problem—the breakdown of communication in our relationship—we had a chance to work together to find answers.

I found out that Leslie wanted more freedom. I had turned down her request to go to an event because I wasn't sure of all the details. She was hurt because she had no intention of doing anything wrong. She thought I didn't trust her. This made her angry, because she had proven that she was responsible enough to make good decisions. The more she thought about it, the angrier she became. Leslie felt I was treating her like a child. Once we talked, I let her know that I appreciated the fact that she caused me no worries and that I trusted her completely. She immediately let down her guard as we made a plan that would give her greater freedom but would also open up the lines of communication so we both understood what was going on.

Our goal in these parenting classes became to focus on the situation from every vantage point, to include our teens in the discussions, and to work on our relationships rather than focusing on the symptoms. As the classes progressed, I continued to apply this to my own parenting. I tried to actively listen and work with my teens to strengthen our relationships. If something came up, I talked to them about it rather than mentally developing a list of offenses. All three of my teens noticed how much I had "improved" by leading the parenting class. I had started the class to fix my daughter, but I was the one who was changed. When we quit leading the cell groups, my son would kid me if I started to stray and focus on the wrong things: "Mom, don't you think you ought to get those groups going again? I think you might need a refresher course."

WHEN YOUR TEEN IS RESPONSIBLE

I have made some bad choices in my life, but my parents can't really help me with them. They were my choices to make, and if they could help, I'd let them, but they can't.

Tim B., age 16

If your teen has broken your relationship and is rebelling, the steps in this book will help you. Every aspect—from listening, to communicating, to setting family guidelines and boundaries and consequences, to unconditional love and unceasing prayer—will help you maintain consistency in spite of your teen's attitude or actions. You can moderate your teen's behavior within the home and set expectations for how he will treat you and other members of the family. You can focus on your relationship with God and grow in your personal walk so that your teen can see God in you. Your role is to remain constant until he is willing to change.

I wanted to break their rules and did. I suppose it was my fault, but I was eighteen, and I thought I could make my own decisions for my life.

Brianne S., age 20

If your teen does not change, remember that when she rejects God and his plan for her life, that doesn't mean that she has rejected you. These are two separate issues. She has been given the freedom to choose when to serve God. You will be her example of faith and strength as she finds her way. Pray for her every day. Live and model Christ-like behavior. Don't take her rejection of God personally. When she acts badly, let her take responsibility, but don't let your teen's behavior dictate yours. You can't change her heart, but your response to her can affect the desire for change.

Nineteen-year-old David's mother attended church, but his father did not. David's mother was faithful in her relationship with God, but both of her children followed their father's footsteps, deciding that God wasn't an option. The oldest daughter became pregnant and married right out of high school. David attended church for a while but slipped away. Soon he was hanging out with guys from school and partying, which included smoking weed. David said that his mother did not give up on him and his sister. She offered extravagant love and acceptance to her family. "When I walk in the door, I can count on my mom smiling. She's genuine. She lifts everybody up around her. When I think about God, I think about my mom," David said. Though he is not serving God yet, David is not far away from making a decision, because his mom's constant walk of faith shows him that God is real.

If I'm struggling, tell them to make sure and allow me to know that they still care for me, no matter what, and to pray for me too, of course.

Adam D., age 18

Never Give Up Hope

One father shared his dilemma with me. He had always had a close relationship with his sons but was worried because his daughter was so busy that they rarely talked. He wondered if his daughter even needed him. Later I overheard his daughter talking about her parents. She said, "I love my mom, but my dad is truly my hero. I love him so much." This father had no idea how his daughter felt.

The greatest gift we can give ourselves is hope. We never know what is just around the corner for our teens and for us. It's easy to be blinded by our circumstances and forget the promises of God. He loves your teen more than you do. He has promised to never leave us or disown us, so make God a partner in the healing process.

All the teens I've spoken with desire relationships with their moms and dads. They were willing to forgive and move forward, but most weren't sure how. Sometimes we see only half the picture. We fail to realize that, to teens, we are their heroes.

MAKE IT REAL

Relationship Review

Have I focused on the symptoms rather than the relationship?

Do I want to fix my teen? Am I open to fixing the relationship instead?

What do I see as the problem in the relationship?

What does my teen say is the problem?

Are there practical steps we can take together to heal our relationship?

If I'm the cause of the broken relationship, have I been honest about my role in causing pain?

Have I asked for forgiveness from my teen?

Have I accepted God's forgiveness? Do I understand that God loves me?

Am I willing to move forward and release the past?

Do I make excuses or justify my behavior?

Do I take it personally when my teen rejects God?

Have I modeled consistent Christ-like behavior?

Am I spending personal time with God every day to find the strength, comfort, and joy that I need?

Have I told my teen today that I love him? Have I smiled at him today? Have I touched my teen today (a hug, a touch on the shoulder, or a hand just to connect with him physically)?

I Know That You Hear Me: A Prayer

Precious heavenly Father, I know that you hear me when I call. I lift my relationship with my teen up to you and ask for your divine guidance. Help me to see the whole picture. Help me to hear the heart and cry of my teen if he is hurting. Forgive me for any part I have played in this, and thank you for new beginnings. I know that this is your specialty. You can take the shattered pieces of our lives and put them back together. You make all things new.

I ask that you help me to extend extravagant love to my family. Not insincere words or poorly motivated efforts, but a genuine love that only comes from you. Help me to forgive the debts I have against those who have hurt me. Help me to seek forgiveness from those I have harmed. I release my past and every wounded emotion to you. I don't want them anymore. They are not mine to carry. I ask that you replace those hurts with joy, peace, and a love that overflows out of my life.

If my teen is far from you, I pray that you will compel him to return to you. Protect him, guide him, and watch over him. And remind him of your love. Put people in his path who will guide him back to you. Let me be an example. Help me to be consistent.

I pray that when I want to make my teen's decisions or behaviors a personal issue, you will remind me how many times I have failed you—and yet how much you still love me.

Chapter Twelve

If I Could Tell You One Thing

I have found the paradox that if I love until it hurts, then there is no hurt, but only more love.

—Mother Teresa

Question: If you could tell your parent one thing, what would it be?

We've talked about a lot of issues. Teens poured out their thoughts as they shared with their parents and with me what they need, but we saved the best question for last. A person's last words are usually the most important. Everything that is trivial is pushed to the side as loved ones share the one thing they want you to carry in your heart after they are gone. So I asked the teens to tell me what they would tell their parents if they could say only one thing. What would be the most important words this generation has to say to moms and dads?

The answers were simple and consistent: *Be patient with me. Thank you for caring. I love you.* The overall message was that your teen loves you and needs you in her life. Here are the last words from hundreds of teens spoken directly into the hearts of parents.

I'M TRYING

I'd tell them that I try really hard not to make mistakes.
Hannah N., age 15

Teens want you to know that they are young and make mistakes, but they are really trying. Their desire is to please you. They are still on a learning curve. There are times when they are just as frustrated with their mistakes as you are—perhaps more—because they feel like failures when they let you down. Teens hope that you see the things that they do right and that you will help them as they grow into young adults. They may not ask for it, but they hope for your support.

Teens are looking for people to believe in them, and you, as a parent, are the best person for the job. They are also looking for someone to talk to, and they hope it might be you. They know that you have answers, but they aren't sure how to talk to you because the problems seem so big.

I have a problem that I have recently started to overcome through Christ. I have wanted to tell you since the first day—five years of wasted time and energy.
Travis R., age 18

Your teen hopes that when you look at him you will see a work in progress but also a promise of what is to come.

Don't Be So Hard on Yourself

Just because I'm not perfect doesn't mean that you failed at parenting. There is no one set way to parent. You've done well, and I love you. Thank you.

Sarah H., age 15

Teens want parents to know that they recognize your efforts. If you are trying to parent your teen to the best of your ability, he understands that. You might make a mistake once in a while, but that's okay because he'll probably make a mistake or two himself. What teens don't want is for you to judge yourself based on their actions. Your teen may not tell you, but she thinks you're doing a great job. She's listening to what you are saying, even if she is doing the opposite.

In all honesty, I want to do what's right and aim to do it, but I am a teenager, and part of growing up is making mistakes along the way and learning from them. You've always been my biggest prayer warriors, and through my rebellious stage, I think that's what kept me safe.

Beth R., age 17

Many of the teens *have* made mistakes. They want you to know that the family guidelines—you know, the ones they said were ridiculous and that they hated—kept them safe, even though they intensely disliked them and you at the time. The older teens who were in college had a better grasp of this than some of the younger teens, but for the most part all of the teenagers wanted you to lighten up on yourself every once in a while and take some credit for what you've done right.

I feel you are doing everything right. I can see Jesus shining through you every day. Situations aren't always easy, but I think you handle it well. It's more about me changing, not you.

Teddi H., age 13

I APPRECIATE YOU

I appreciate you, even when I forget to show it.

Jenny M., age 19

Tons of teens said that if they could only say one thing, they would let their parents know that they appreciate the tough job that parents have. Most of them understood that parenting is a selfless task. They understand how hard it is for you to have to be the bad guy all the time.

I appreciate what you are trying to do even though I don't like it.

Linda S., age 14

They recognize the fact that they don't always make it easy for you. It's normal for teens to try to stretch and grow and push the boundaries as you pull and tug to keep them safe. They know that you are trying to decide how far to let them go and where to draw the lines. Many teens understand it's a balancing act. They're teens, and they want freedom, but they do appreciate the fact that you love them enough to help them navigate life and make decisions as they mature. They appreciate the fact that it's hard to let go, and they love it when you trust them enough to let them take a step forward on their own. More than anything, they appreciate you.

Even though I don't always think you are right, you really are, and I should give you the credit you deserve.

Jennifer L., age 15

Thank You for Caring

Several teens thought it was awesome that a parent would care enough to want to hear what they had to say. One teen said that she was already reading parenting books so that she could one day be a good parent. She said it encouraged her that her mom continued to grow as a parent even though she was leaving for college the next year.

I'd tell them that I love them and thank them for every little thing that they have done for me. I think I have grown up to be a good person.

Allison L., age 20

Reading a parenting book is one way to show that you care, but teens said that their parents demonstrated that they cared in a thousand different ways. When the children were little, it was kisses on their scraped fingers or running after a bike as you taught them how to ride a two-wheeler without killing themselves. Now it's staying up to make sure he comes in safe, even though you are tired. It's fixing lasagna with real ricotta cheese because your teen loves it, even though you are on a diet and have to eat tuna on wheat. It's stepping over her clothes on the bathroom floor for the fiftieth time and being patient as you teach her how to be responsible for her own dirty socks. It's filling out financial aid papers. It's attending ball games in subzero weather. It's driving around town with a new driver who is still trying to figure out the brakes from the gas pedal. It's driving him to college for the first time and putting on your best face, then crying all the way home because you already miss him.

I love it when you pray with me, because it shows that you care. You love God so much. You are the ones who got me to go to church and prayed the prayer of God with me. I don't feel like a clone, but I'm spiritually like you, Mom. You help me to be spiritual.

Derek H., age 16

They appreciate the fact that you guide them spiritually. Some teens said that it was their moms or dads who introduced them to Christ, who made God real to them, who made their homes a place where God existed.

They know that we do this because we care. It works for Richard and me because we love our children and we love being a part of their lives. It works for your teen as well. One day she will take what she has learned from your example and apply it to her own children. Won't it be fun to watch?

They are great examples. They are both Christians and show it in their lifestyle. I am truly blessed to have awesome Christian parents.

Elizabeth H., age 14

I Would Tell Them that I Love Them

I'd tell them that I love them and thank them for the awesome godly example they have shown me in their own lives.

Ricky M., age 16

The most common answer to this question contained three little words: *I love you.* Teens, even those who were angry or frustrated or felt that their relationship needed work, said the one thing they wanted their parents to know was that they love them. Many teens described their parents as their best friends.

If I could tell my mom one thing it would be that I love her more than words could ever say and that she's my best friend. If I could tell my dad one thing, it would be that I love him and forgive him, though I'm not ready to have him back in my life yet.

Mika W., age 17

Teens whose relationships with their parents were nonexistent or struggling still wanted to let their parents know that love was the foundation of their relationships. Teens like Mika, whose father is an alcoholic, love their parents regardless. Though Mika set boundaries, she hoped that one day her father would become what she called an "ideal dad." Yet, in spite of everything, she still loved him and said that her last words to him would be of love and forgiveness.

I hope that you realize that your teen loves you. I pray that this book and the thoughts that hundreds of teens shared will spur you on to see that you are an important part of your own teen's life. Why? Because she loves you—and that's reason enough!

I love you, every time!

Louise C., age 16

NOTES

1 Alan Guttmacher Institute, "Facts in Brief: Sexually Transmitted Diseases in the United States," September 1993, http://www.agi-usa.org/index.html.

2 "Analysis of the Causes of Decline in the Non-Marital Birth and Pregnancy Rates for Teens from 1991 to 1995," *Adolescent and Family Health* 3, no. 1, <http://www.physconsortium.com/pdfs/afh_journal_paper.pdf>.

3 "Attitudes Become More Negative on Abortion," *The Buffalo News*, November 27, 2002. Information from Zogby International Poll, November 12–14, 2002, http://www.zogby.com/.

4 Cool, Lisa Collier, "Secret Sex Lives of Kids," *Ladies Home Journal*, March 2001, p. 156.

5 Arlene Saluter, "Marital Status and Living Arrangements," U.S. Bureau of the Census, series P20–484 (March 1996), p. vi.

6 <http://www.barna.org/cgi-bin/PageCategory.asp?CategoryID=37>. Barna Research Group, Ventura, Calif.

7 Barna, George, "Faith and Spirituality," *Real Teens: A Contemporary Snapshot of Youth Culture* (Ventura, Calif.: Regal, 2001), p. 121.

8 "Of Parents and Grandparents," *New York Times*, January 16, 2000, p. 16.

9 Princeton Survey Research Associates. "Speaking of Kids: A National Survey of Children and Parents." Sponsored by the National Commission on Children.

10 Kaufman, P., Chen, X., Choy, S. P., et al., *Indicators of School Crime and Safety: 2001.* U.S. Departments of

Education and Justice. NCES 2002. 113/NCJ-190075. Washington, DC: 2001, p. iii.

11 Data provided in National Center for Health Statistics, GMWK291 Death Rates for 72 Selected Causes by 5-Year Age Groups, Race, and Sex: United States, 1979–98, p. 485. Centers for Disease Control and Prevention.

12 Centers for Disease Control and Prevention, WISQARS (Web-based Injury Statistics Query and Reporting System).

T. Suzanne Eller is the author of *Real Teens, Real Stories, Real Life* and ministers to teens around the world through http://daretobelieve.org, a website devoted to sharing real stories, devos, and poetry written for and by teens. Suzanne is a popular speaker to teens and parents of teens. She can be reached at tseller@daretobelieve.org.

The Word at Work . . .

What would you do if you wanted to share God's love with children on the streets of your city? That's the dilemma David C. Cook faced in 1870s Chicago. His answer was to create literature that would capture children's hearts.

Out of those humble beginnings grew a worldwide ministry that has used literature to proclaim God's love and disciple generation after generation. Cook Communications Ministries is committed to personal discipleship—to helping people of all ages learn God's Word, embrace his salvation, walk in his ways, and minister in his name.

Opportunities—and Crisis

We live in a land of plenty—including plenty of Christian literature! But what about the rest of the world? Jesus commanded, "Go and make disciples of all nations" (Matt. 28:19) and we want to obey this commandment. But how does a publishing organization "go" into all the world?

There are five times as many Christians around the world as there are in North America. Christian workers in many of these countries have no more than a New Testament, or perhaps a single shared copy of the Bible, from which to learn and teach.

We are committed to sharing what God has given us with such Christians.

A vital part of Cook Communications Ministries is our international outreach, Cook Communications Ministries International (CCMI). Your purchase of this book, and of other books and Christian-growth products from Cook, enables CCMI to provide Bibles and Christian literature to people in more than 150 languages in 65 countries.

Cook Communications Ministries is a not-for-profit, self-supporting organization. Revenues from sales of our books, Bible curriculum, and other church and home products not only fund our U.S. ministry, but also fund our CCMI ministry around the world. One hundred percent of donations to CCMI go to our international literature programs.

. . . Around the World

CCMI reaches out internationally in three ways:

- Our premier International Christian Publishing Institute (ICPI) trains leaders from nationally led publishing houses around the world to develop evangelism and discipleship materials to transform lives in their countries.

- We provide literature for pastors, evangelists, and Christian workers in their national language. We provide study helps for pastors and lay leaders in many parts of the world, such as China, India, Cuba, Iran, and Vietnam.

- We reach people at risk—refugees, AIDS victims, street children, and famine victims—with God's Word. CCMI puts literature that shares the Good News into the hands of people at spiritual risk—people who might die before they hear the name of Jesus and are transformed by his love.

Word Power—God's Power

Faith Kidz, RiverOak, Honor, Life Journey, Victor, NexGen — every time you purchase a book produced by Cook Communications Ministries, you not only meet a vital personal need in your life or in the life of someone you love, but you're also a part of ministering to José in Colombia, Humberto in Chile, Gousa in India, or Lidiane in Brazil. You help make it possible for a pastor in China, a child in Peru, or a mother in West Africa to enjoy a life-changing book. And because you helped, children and adults around the world are learning God's Word and walking in his ways.

Thank you for your partnership in helping to disciple the world. May God bless you with the power of his Word in your life.

For more information about our international ministries, visit www.ccmi.org.